**THE Incentives and Rewards HAND-BOOK**

A summary of bonus opportunities in different companies

Bo Jäghult

Contributing Editor Greg Mathers

Copyright © 2022

ISBN: 978-1-952587-24-5

*Inquiries:*

Bo@jagult.se

Greg@adizes.com

Publisher: 1212 Mark Ave,

Carpinteria, CA 93013, United States

Email: publishing@adizes.com

Website: **https://publications.adizes.com**

# INCENTIVES AND REWARDS

By Bo Jäghult

## A practical handbook on bonuses in organizations

*Contributing editor*
*Greg Mathers*

# CONTENTS

# INTRODUCTION

Over the last 20 years, managers have increasingly found it necessary to provide extra financial rewards for effective managers and clever co-workers. These rewards run the gamut from commissions to specific project bonuses, to company shares and share options. Money has almost always been the first-choice tool for trying to motivate people, but is money really the first-place motivation people take from work?

Of course, we know that is not the case. People are equally or more motivated by interesting work, a good working environment, capable and professional co-workers, and new and challenging tasks. Therefore, in this book I will focus both on financial and non-financial rewards.

The many managers I have been fortunate enough to work with have ranged from being bright, fast thinking and extremely capable to being young and inexperienced. Across this range I have found virtually all of them have a great interest in trying to find the right mix and amount of rewards to better motivate their people. In their quest to create a motivating rewards system, managers often make several mistakes.

The rewards are sometimes paltry, sometimes extreme and appear to be arbitrary. Often, clear connections between the reward and the important results needed for the company are not obvious.

Short-term results, which often are the basis for the rewards, are prioritized, while neglecting long-term development and change

In this book, I will show how to use rewards to both stimulate efforts on short-term results and encourage activity on long-term growth and development. I will cover how reward programs can be constructed, as well as what is going to be rewarded; how much the reward should be and what types of rewards you can use.

I primarily started this as a book on financial rewards, but it quickly became obvious I should also focus on the fact that people also get a high degree of motivation from more than just money. For that reason, the first third of the book is about "intrinsic rewards." Praise, new challenges, training and learning opportunities, and personal development are a few examples of intrinsic motivators. With "intrinsic rewards" people get excited about something other than money. The remainder of the book will be on different types of financial rewards and reward systems.

My own primary reward will be that someone reads this handbook and eventually finds at least one valuable idea.


Sweden 2020
Bo Jäghult

# 1. REWARDS IN COMPANIES

The systems of rewards in companies often drive conflict.

Think for a moment how employees view their compensation. The perception tends to be that salary is received for doing just what they were employed to do. After all, why should an employee do more if he is not rewarded more? But when people do perform it is not always clear what constitutes good results or what is meant by an extra reward.

Managers, though, often have another view on compensation; salary should be enough for an employee to do whatever is asked of her and no extra money should be needed. These different expectations can and do create a lot of tension.

Many companies offer variable compensation, rewards, or bonuses. Often, bonuses will be the same for everyone. However, people receiving a bonus would like to earn extra based on their individual contribution. Sometimes a simple pat on the back might be enough, but many expect a financial reward.

Managers expect financial rewards to elicit behavior considered good for the organization. Rewards are the tools by which managers try to motivate their employees. But should this be the primary use of financial rewards? After all, do managers hire unmotivated people who need to be motivated, or is something else going on that causes people to lose their motivation over time?

Managers also use "psychological rewards", such as praise, recognition, more responsibility, and participation in different kinds of decisions. We call these intrinsic rewards.

Of course, intrinsic rewards are not always enough, and people do need to get something in their wallets. Such financial incentives are called extrinsic rewards and include bonuses, commissions, or profit sharing, as well as special arrangements like options and shares of ownership. As for what the mix of intrinsic and extrinsic rewards should be, experience (and research) shows that more than 50 percent of motivation in working life comes from the availability of intrinsic rewards.

While managers understand the necessity to find what behaviors the organization needs to emphasize and reinforce, sometimes less clear is that different people expect and respond to different types of rewards.

When setting out to construct a reward system you first need to understand what behaviors are already being rewarded in your organization. Realize that even without a formal reward system there are behaviors being reinforced by management and owners, consciously and unconsciously. A perceived acknowledgment or rebuff in a manager's attitude or behavior is often enough to reinforce or dampen behavior.

Rewards come in many forms. As we move through this book you will see different terms like incentive, bonus, or reward. These all should be understood as a form of compensation in *addition* to a fixed salary meant as positive reinforcement. This additional reward can be either financial or some sort of positive acknowledgement and, whenever possible, needs to be for a *specific* result achieved by an individual or a group.

We also want to look at the question, how important are these incentives? Are they effective because we mainly work in anticipation of being paid, or do we work because we enjoy working and, if so, how should this affect a reward system?

To be a judge of this it is useful to look at your own achievements and compare. What have you done that gave you great satisfaction? When did you feel you had accomplished something worthwhile? Was it when you received a large financial pay-out, or was it the actual result you achieved? Whatever your answer, it is important to feel satisfaction and pride in your accomplishments and to be rewarded for your efforts.

# 2. WHY GIVE REWARDS?

Why do we give rewards? Are rewards truly necessary? What about when employees have salaries that are already more or less equal to their tasks?

I want to give some ideas and reasons why it makes good business sense to give extra compensation - a bonus – or some special recognition in connection with completing certain tasks and achieving specific results.

## 2.1 TO RECOGNIZE THOSE WHO HAVE EARNED RECOGNITION

There are key people who have a greater impact on a company's results. Certainly, it may be the CEO or others in top management. But it can also be salespeople working with important products in key markets, scientists whose results are crucial to new innovations, or a host of other people in important positions.

Many of the executives we see rewarded in the media – and not always in a positive way – are global traders in funds, shares or other financial instruments. The unusually large bonuses we read about raise questions about how performance is really measured. While these people can influence a company's financial fortunes, they seem to have little effect on a company's operations, and they do not always bring a positive message about rewards.

## 2.2 TO DIRECT PEOPLE'S EFFORTS TOWARDS AREAS OF IMPORTANCE TO THE COMPANY

A company's CEO is often rewarded, if a reward system exists, based on the overall result of the company. Results are measured by the movement of the share price, the growth of equity, tracking company profits, or any number of other options.

Other managers and key people in such a system may also be rewarded based on such measurable results linked to key outcomes of the company. For these "Key Performance Indicators" or KPIs to be effective, the person whose performance is measured against them must be able to impact them. Then, the KPIs can be used to evaluate the performance level for any extra compensation.

Unfortunately, this is not always the case. Managers tend to measure and reward certain areas because it has always been done that way, or they have seen it done elsewhere as a "best practice." Revenue, net margin, gross profit, personnel turnover are interesting and important measurements. However, the person being evaluated cannot always influence these results to any great extent. This leads to a lot of frustration. Also, it is often the case that many measured tasks are not even the issues of most importance for the company.

For example, should we put the greatest weight on revenue growth for a company that has steadily been losing money for the last 3 years? Of course, it depends. If losses are due to investments in a failed project, then it might make sense. If the losses are due to poor utilization of resources, then management should probably be tracking other, more important performance indicators.

## 2.3 AND TO REINFORCE BEHAVIOR SO THAT EMPLOYEES DO MORE OF THE IMPORTANT TASKS

One reason why management rewards certain performance and certain people is *they want more of the same*. Lacking other ideas or solutions, managers introduce rewards in the form of money in the hope that key people will understand that it pays off to continue to do well in specific areas.

## REFLECTIONS

When you follow media reports as I do around rewards and bonuses, you see much interest concerning the amount of payments but very little interest in why someone gets an extra payment.

During one twelve-month period, I collected 110 newspaper and magazine articles around rewards and bonuses. Eighty of the articles covered rewards to top management – mostly CEO´s. The other articles were mostly about bonuses in public administration or to employees in banks and other industries but connection, or rather the lack of connection, between financial rewards and performance was almost never mentioned. Nothing, well nearly nothing, was written about why someone got an extra reward.

Also, the performance measurement method and the basis for the reward were not mentioned at all. There was sometimes a comment that the reward to the CEO was a result of the development of the share price or its development compared to the competitors. Otherwise, nothing.

# 3. SOME ARGUE EXTRA REWARDS ARE NOT REALLY NEEDED

In this next section we look at arguments against rewards. There are many self-proclaimed experts that believe variable payment for key people should not exist. Why?

## 3.1 "YOU CANNOT MEASURE WHAT IS TRULY IMPORTANT"

Without any doubt there are many key areas and tasks within a company that are difficult to measure.

Just a few examples are:

- Increased customer satisfaction
- The quality in our sales calls
- The result of our last marketing campaign
- The result of our management training
- The move of our head office
- The implementation of our new computer process

We can continue this list, maybe not forever, but at least quite a long time. Of course, the list of these activities differs depending on the industry and which key person we are talking about.

When exploring performance measurement techniques, realize that it is not always necessary to measure in financial terms, i.e., revenues, profits, costs, etc. Often more important is to measure the client's response in a customer survey, whether a certain activity has occurred or not, or if certain activities are improving a process.

A useful rule of thumb is to "measure approximately" those activities and results that are important rather than to measure precisely what is not so important. Even more vital is to not base rewards on results the employee has little ability to impact.

Often the measurement will be simple verification, an either or discussion. *Have we completed this activity or not?*

- Do we have a new computer process or not?
- Did the new customer brochure get printed on time or not?
- Did we implement the new sales training or not?

We cannot always measure the effects of a sales training. But at least we can know if it took place. These are so called "binary" results, meaning they either happen or do not happen and will be discussed more in chapter 7 on different types of rewards.

## 3.2 "YOU DO NOT ALWAYS KNOW WHAT IS MOST IMPORTANT TO BE DOING RIGHT NOW"

A crucial premise for a successful reward system is that we know, "what are the important activities to be pursuing at any given time?" This question needs to be at the forefront of our thinking and our design efforts: "Do we really know what we should be doing right now?"

The answer is often yes, but sometimes no. We live in times of accelerated change and the priorities we face are constantly shifting. What is important this year often does not have the same importance next year.

Rewards need to align with the current organizational priorities. Those priorities are diverse and ever evolving. The implication, then, is that reward systems need to be constantly shifting and evolving as well. One of the greatest risks is that we get stuck in a reward system that once was working but no longer fits the current environment.

What should also be obvious – but is not always adequately thought through – is that different individuals with different positions are saddled with different and shifting priorities. Often our people are linked through the structure and so are measured from the same base and rewarded similarly even though they have very different conditions and demands. This is another source of frustration needing resolution.

## 3.3 "INDIVIDUALS SHOULD HAVE A GOOD BASE SALARY, SO THEY DO NOT NEED ANY EXTRA REWARD AND THIS SHOULD BE ESPECIALLY TRUE FOR TOP MANAGEMENT"

Opponents to rewards often have the opinion – as is pointed out in the title above – that the base salary should be at such a level that no extra payments are needed. This argument is mostly used concerning top management. The contention is that managers pursuing these extra rewards will be tempted to take actions that in the short run benefit themselves rather than the future of the company.

An example is a company which established a goal to generate greater liquidity and tied a top management reward to achieving the goal. At the end of the year top management simply sold certain valuable assets and improved the liquidity considerably. As a result, they received the agreed bonus, but selling those assets was not in the long-term interest of the company.

## 3.4 "PEOPLE SOMETIMES GET OFFENDED WHEN THEY BELIEVE YOU ARE TRYING TO BRIBE THEM THROUGH REWARDS."

People for the most part understand on their own what is the right action to take for the health of the company. When a manager comes in and is trying to direct a person's activities through a reward in the same direction as the individual is already going, he can be perceived both positively and negatively. Positive in that you get something extra for something you already are doing, and you know is the right thing.

But sometimes you feel your manager did not believe you were smart enough to realize the right way on your own and that he or she must step in and teach you and motivate you in the right direction with the help of money. This can be quite disheartening.

## 3.5 "MOTIVATION COMES FROM FIXING DISSATISFACTION"

Here is a basic problem about motivation and dissatisfaction that managers have gotten wrong for as long as management has been around. We believe that by improving things employees are complaining about, they will respond with greater motivation.

However, this is seldom the case. Complaints and dissatisfaction often focus on unsatisfactory working conditions, unfair situations and similar. But removing the source of dissatisfaction only means that the wrong situation is removed, and some sort of acceptable or normal situation is established. This does not provide motivation. Instead, "this is how it should have been all the time" is often the type of response you will hear.

One comfort you might take though, is that until you remove the source of dissatisfaction you likely will not have a large impact with activities that are motivating. So, if we do not first take care of the dissatisfiers, instilling activities and systems we feel should be motivating might not get a good response.

*Remember, removing a source of dissatisfaction does not motivate people. It only makes them less dissatisfied.*

# 4. HOW DO WE REWARD PEOPLE?

We are always rewarding behavior in some way – in all organizations – either consciously or unconsciously. The question is how do we become more conscious of what we are doing and continue to do it better? When working to keep people motivated, ask these questions.

- Do we have explicit connections to the company's goals?
- Do we set goals that are measurable, or do we use more subjective or random goals?
- Are we using punishments, not physical punishments, but maybe a demeaning attitude or disparaging criticism?
- Is risk-taking promoted and rewarded correctly for pursuing and achieving goals?

Throughout this book when we talk about rewards, they are always connected with a result or accomplishment which is *known and agreed upon in advance*. This means that the reward is not dependent on a manger's reaction to an activity. The reward is not decided on after the result is known and it will not be distributed at the manager's discretion. *The reward should be distributed only for the results and in the amount agreed upon in advance.*

Maybe an employee has performed well and a reward is justified. For this type of situation I recommend a reactive reward called recognition. Recognition can be in the form of a verbal congratulation individually or in front of a group or it could be with the presentation of some type of award. But you should not start the practice of giving unplanned financial rewards. If you do so, you will build the expectations that for everything extra someone does there will be money.

You should save the financial rewards for reaching planned performance with goals because knowing in advance that the reward is available is important for motivation. For unexpected valuable performance, positive recognition is often enough and can take the form of public praise, positive recommendations, and continued inclusion in future important projects.

Years of research and experience has shown that intrinsic rewards have the greatest effect on improving motivation. Still, for many individuals in the company financial rewards are also motivating and can engage employees in producing better and more efficient work; this, of course, is one of the most important reasons to offer rewards.

The purpose of rewards is not limited to improving efficiency and results. Increased well-being and the will to stay longer in the company are also positive side-effects.

*You cannot take a reward – only be given one.*

## 4.1 HOW CAN INCENTIVES BE USED IN COMPANIES?

With experience, we have seen that various incentives plus positive feedback create positive minded individuals who produce greater efforts and better results. Just the possibility of receiving a financial reward increases motivation. This is true for individuals as well as groups.

In business, extra pay, more spare time or other forms of incentives are given for good performance. Most of us feel good when we receive these incentives and would like it to happen again. But is this all there is to the concept of incentives? Or is there something more?

Maybe not necessarily something more, but surely we can agree that there are ulterior motives for rewarding other people. We might show approval to others simply because it feels good; but it is also possible that people who show approval to others have hidden agendas. Perhaps we show approval because we want to encourage someone to do something he or she did not contemplate doing. And there might be something that a manager wants to affect in a more wanted direction.

There are several possible reasons to give incentives. Here are a few legitimate examples:

- To get people to work harder
- To create motivation so individuals and groups feel good
- To assure that key people remain in the organization
- To reward and institutionalize efficiency
- To increase one's own feeling of competence as a leader

Often companies claim they do not have any formal system of incentives. This may be partly true, but all companies do have some sort of a system for rewards, even if they do not realize it.

In many small to medium sized companies, there often is no formal reward system. However, you can always find that a certain pattern exists to rewarding and punishing behavior: *"This is the way we do things; this is a good result, and we would like to see more of it."*

To accept and understand the statement that all organizations have a reward system, we must have an accepted understanding of what incentives and incentive systems are all about.

Recognition is a type of incentive. Besides cash, recognition may be one of the most important incentives. Or maybe the most important one!

The question is: Do you have to give an extra financial reward to motivate people? This leads to another question – do people require an additional financial incentive to produce good results?

If we believe that to be the case, we must be prepared to pay more to get more - but is this correct?

I will try to answer that question.

# 5. DIFFERENT TYPES OF REWARDS

Some people believe in motivating mainly through financial rewards. Some think motivation should come from sources other than financial rewards.

Personally, I believe we should use a combination of financial and non-financial rewards.

I will focus on three types of rewards. We need to find and work with the right type to coincide with the desired results. In my experience, financial rewards are not the primary type nor always the place to start.

Three types of rewards

- Individual needs / the job itself
- Non-financial rewards / Praise, new challenges
- Financial rewards / money, shares, options

When developing rewards, a seemingly obvious starting point is financial rewards. However, we first need to recognize that the work in and of itself should be a rewarding experience. When people are not fulfilled through their work, they will ask for more financial rewards to fill that hole.

## 5.1 THE FIRST TYPE OF REWARD: MY OWN NEEDS AND THE JOB ITSELF

If you as an employee see a future that you like, and you engage in tasks that you feel are important, motivation will naturally follow. A job that is important for the company but also important for you will stimulate your efforts. This should reduce the focus on greater amounts of money as a primary motivator.

If you can create the right job and make it more meaningful for your employees, they will also experience the same motivating affect as above and should also have a reduced focus on money as a primary motivator.

This means, when possible, you need to create a job that is in and of itself motivating. Being able to do this requires you design a job, so a person feels:

- My job is meaningful
- My competence is used
- I have possibilities to choose how to work
- I am learning new things
- I am developing myself

## MY JOB FEELS MEANINGFUL

A job feels meaningful when you can see a future you like, and you are able to engage in tasks you feel are important. While the work is important for the company, you also need to feel it is important to you.

Can we as responsible managers add more meaning to the jobs for our employees? Of course, it is possible. The problem arises when I have many people reporting to me, and all have different opinions of what is important and meaningful in their work.

A young, new employee might think her new tasks are meaningful, while a more experienced colleague could think the same tasks are basic and is seeking different challenges.

## USING MY COMPETENCE

Using your competence makes you feel more useful and increases your self-esteem. Also, when you are stretched to use all your knowledge to complete your tasks, you feel you are growing. To support your work, you should get continuous verbal feedback about how you perform.

By having interesting challenges which you must solve, you will develop. This assumes that you have the competence to take responsibility for bigger and more complex tasks and have the freedom to do so without interference from others. With this you can feel that your own competence is used and growing. People want a challenge in what they are doing.

## I SHOULD BE ABLE TO CHOOSE HOW I COMPLETE A TASK.

Completing a delegated task from A to D

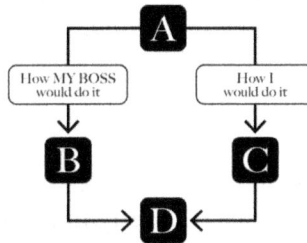

You should have the possibility to choose how you complete your tasks.

When starting at point A and tasked with reaching objective D as shown in the diagram above, it is often difficult for others to see that by going from A to C you will still reach the point D just as well as if you go via B. This is especially true if it was your boss expecting you to go through point B and you choose point C instead.

Your possibility to follow your own conviction means a lot for your own satisfaction and motivation. Many managers interfere too early when a subordinate uses a different approach, and this builds frustration.

We seldom know the optimal way to achieve an objective until it is completed. Just because we previously approached and solved problems successfully using certain methods does not mean those methods are still the best.

To allow someone to test and pursue her own way is challenging, but people need to be somewhat self-directed, and it also just may result in a better way.

## I CAN DEVELOP MYSELF

You develop yourself and your self-confidence when you feel engaged and feel responsibility for your actions. This is possible when you have full information about the task and its purpose. When you have this, and you can choose your own path to solve the task - the path you believe in - then you will feel you have control and know what is happening.

In this situation, you can constantly follow the progress of your work in the scope of bigger projects and objectives. You can see the success as it emerges and your role in driving that success. You develop yourself as the project progresses.

Again, it is very much about you being able to act according to how you think a task should be accomplished – to choose your own way; to be responsible and act on your own conviction.

## CONCLUSIONS

The path to creating a reward could be viewed as a staircase with understanding personal competencies and designing the job with some level of self-direction as the first step. For various reasons, we often start our development of rewards in different places.

There are financial and non-financial ways of being rewarded and both approaches should be used to structure rewards. Managers tend to focus mostly on financial rewards when the job is fulfilled – but it is often not necessary for management to use financial rewards and employees are often ready to take on tasks they feel are important without financial incentives.

Of course, it is not easy to design a reward system such that each person feels the right level of challenge and that his or her development needs are being adequately addressed. Complicating this is the fact that the needs of everyone are different.

To make our lives easier, we tend to rely on financial rewards and often ignore the other needs. But, by doing so we risk missing the strongest motivators available; self-direction and control over your situation, the desire to improve and master a job, and the feeling of contributing to something larger than yourself.

So, what is the best? What should we use? Job satisfaction or money? The answer is not so easy.

By asking managers - and I have been doing it for decades: "Which tools are best to use if you want to motivate employees?" The answer is usually "financial rewards"

Okay, the next question "What motivates you in your job?"

The answer from a manager will usually be:

*"New challenges, expanded responsibility, new tasks etc."*

Money does not seem to be the real driving force when people answer about themselves. So, what is it in your case? Do you feel motivation comes from more money or from the job itself?

One final question:

*"What do you think motivates your employees?"*

The answer from managers again is money. We tend to believe that others have a different driving interest than we have; they are driven by money while we are driven by opportunities for growth, development, and challenge.

My experience is that the most important motivation at work comes from the job being interesting and challenging and that there are individuals and groups I enjoy working with and with whom I can develop together. I have found this applies to all levels of the organization. To varying degrees at different levels we are mostly motivated by an exciting, interesting, and challenging job.

If these elements of the job are lacking, then people request money to fill the gap. They usually will not ask for a more interesting and challenging job because they do not see that as a viable solution. Therefore, it is easier to ask for more money.

Often managers do not believe that their employees are as attuned as themselves to the fact that money might not be a primary motivation factor.

Of course, it is not easy to find the right elements of job satisfaction for each person that also align with the company.

Ongoing praise, development and learning can do wonders, but they do have their limitations. Over time, individual needs will change – people develop and get training. Praise may never be too much, but it likely works best in the long run as a complement to other rewards.

So, what do we do? Adhere to the individual's needs by making sure that the job is attractive and interesting.

But here is the rub. It is not always possible to create a job that is challenging and interesting. So, then what should we as managers do?

We need to move to the next step on the ladder of rewards design.

## 5.2 THE SECOND TYPE OF REWARDS:
## NEW RESPONSIBILITIES, PRAISE, AND OTHER CHALLENGES

To ensure employee performance remains relevant, and motivation and productivity stay high over time, means the job must change and develop as conditions are changing and developing. An important tool to achieving this is a well-structured and regular employee performance evaluation and development talk.

Being able to satisfy all of an individual's dreams and desires and thus increase each one's motivation is probably not realistic. But we try to do the best we can. Ask yourself, "do I as a manager responsible for rewarding employees make good faith efforts to create interesting and challenging jobs or do I rely on financial incentives?"

Increased responsibility for new areas, opportunities for development and training, and the chance to organize special occasional events are examples of things that can be interesting and motivating. Some of these, for example sending someone to a specialized training, can be expensive so the boundary between financial and non-financial rewards is not entirely straight-forward.

34

Next, we will explore some tools to help us understand and strengthen certain behaviors in employees. These non-financial tools can help us define better jobs as well as motivate better performance.

Formal and scheduled employee performance evaluations and development talks should be conducted once a year. This "old" tool first gained prominence in the 1970s and now is increasingly a regular practice. The idea is that the manager and each employee meet regularly (often once a year but can be more frequent) and both parties have properly prepared themselves to discuss recent performance levels and future expectations. The meeting could be structured around the following questions.

*"What does the employee need to achieve over the next period?"*

While the question might seem silly or naive, my experience shows that when a manager and an employee separately make a list of what they believe are the employees expected achievements over the next period, the misalignment is significant with often less than 50 percent common understanding of expectations. Of course, if they both do not agree where they are headed there is good chance, they will end up in different places.

*"What is the employee's job content?"*

Managers and employees often have different opinions on what should be done daily. If the manager asks about the employee's perception of his or her tasks, you will often find there is very small agreement with the manager's opinion. See the picture below.

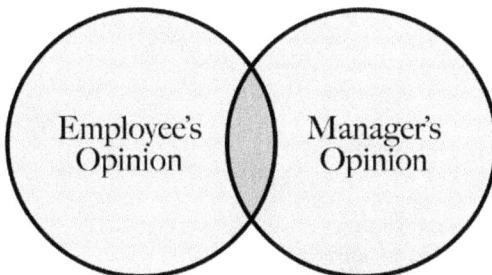

- The shared perception of the work content is often less than 50 percent.
- The ideal is not 100 percent. The manager cannot possibly know all the areas that the employee should perform. But the smaller the overlap the less the boss knows what the employee is doing and the less the employee understands the boss's expectations.

The important thing is to regularly check what each understands as of today and to find common ground.

The next question could be:

*"How has the employee succeeded?"*

An employee may not ask this question, but the manager should answer it proactively. Being told how you have succeeded and having successful results recognized is an essential part of job motivation. You should as often as possible, use concrete examples, which then leads to further discussion.

- Feedback on a result - good or bad - is important and not just concerning the extremes. To only comment on extremely good or bad results is not enough. Comments also about ongoing work, even with typical results keeps people attuned to performance expectations.
- Concrete examples from achieved results are good as a basis for the discussion.
- Regular, periodic discussions are important - whether results are good or bad. How did the results come about?

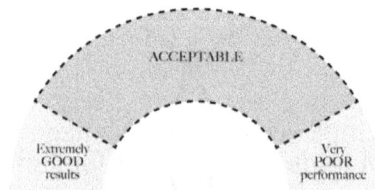

Feedback to employees should focus
on Acceptable results, not only good
or poor performance

Finally, the last question.

*"Which areas should the employee improve?"*

We must maintain a focus on individual development. This means that you should constantly be seeking to "Be relatively as skilled in your work tomorrow as you are today."

This may seem like a daunting task. But when looking at the rate of change in technology and methods, you quickly realize that maintaining relevant skill levels is an ongoing and constant challenge. Unfortunately, we do not always involve older employees in skills development.

To be "relatively as skilled in my work going forward, as I am today", proves to be challenging. Continuous dialogue between the manager and employee helps to ensure that both the present situation and future requirements are mutually understood. This is a prerequisite for continued development and performance, but also impacts the individual's continued motivation.

The left picture on the next page shows that the individual fulfils the requirements of the position well today. After some time, the right picture shows that the requirements for the position have increased while the individual has the same skills as before. A slip occurs where the individual no longer fulfils the job requirements.

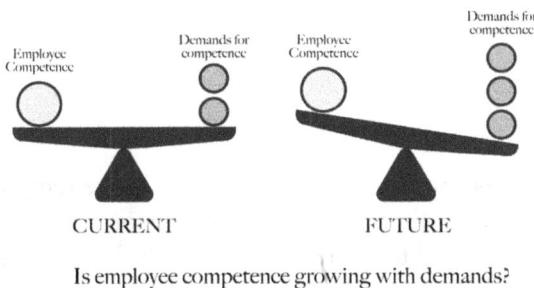

Is employee competence growing with demands?

The definition of individual development should be "To continue to be at least as skilled in my position in the future as I am now."

As job technologies and design constantly change, you need to ask: what should I do to grow my skills and capabilities to maintain my competence?

## THE AVAILABILITY OF NEW RESPONSIBILITIES

The availability of new responsibilities can be a continued source of motivation and it is important, so people have opportunities to continuously develop in their jobs. This can be done in several ways as discussed below.

### Expand the area of responsibility

You can increase an employee's scope of responsibility and authority. This happens naturally when an employee moves to a new position, but you can also expand an existing area of responsibility to help meet this need.

### Temporary responsibilities

You can provide opportunity for development by giving responsibility for a campaign, a conference, a project, or a special event. Contrary to the above, this is not a permanent responsibility but a temporary extension of responsibility.

### Delegation

In both examples above, it is important to delegate temporary or permanent authority. You might also delegate to a person who does not report to you. Of course, you need to coordinate this with the person's manager who needs to be informed about the performance.

The chance to deal with new tasks or new areas of responsibility is challenging for most people and a source of motivation. However, as a manager offering this opportunity you must do it the right way. The new task area must become a real responsibility that you give to the person along with authority for how the task is accomplished.

Often what managers do, is to simply offer more work without any real responsibility, which includes decision-making authority. In such cases, the experience is often the opposite of what you were trying to achieve – disappointment, frustration, and demotivation!

When giving developmental tasks, it is vital that the person is given a significant task with some level control over how the work gets done. "Can you make sure this area is kept clear" is not delegation just another task to accomplish. Nothing is wrong with that per se, but it is not a delegation of responsibility with authority.

## FEEDBACK ON PERFORMANCE

Praise has been studied by numerous researchers looking into whether extra rewards really motivate staff to perform better. One view, relatively agreed upon, is that a reward should be adapted as far as possible to the individual's needs. In some people, money is interesting, in other people you will need to find other motivators. Praise has been found to be a useful motivator.

It is said that praise costs very little. But sometimes it gives more satisfaction than just money. This is especially true if a person already has enough financial compensation.

Praise can be given in many ways. Some of the ways are not as motivating as the praise giver might have hoped for.

Here are some ideas to help you give praise.

- Point out what is positive instead of criticizing what is negative
- Give praise in front of others - criticize in private
- Give your own feedback, do not refer only to what others have said, give your own examples
- Give praise as close as possible to the event. If you cannot give praise immediately, provide feedback very soon
- Link results and praise. Give concrete examples
- Try to praise essential tasks, not trivial things

Too many managers are light with praise. When asked why, many managers offer explanations such as:

"My employees know that I appreciate their efforts - I do not have to bring it up so often."

"It feels fake to offer praise regularly. As if I am trying just to flatter them."

We tend to not give praise as often as we probably should. Instead, managers focus on criticizing what is not working. I recall a manager saying to me, "At the end of the day we have to change what is not working."

Certainly, this is true. But we should not limit ourselves to only commenting on what is wrong. We need to also reinforce good behavior and results. We do this through praise.

*And by the way, praise is motivating for the receiver, but it is also rewarding to give praise!*

## GREATER PARTICIPATION OF EMPLOYEES IN DECISION-MAKING SHOULD BE PART OF A COMPANY'S WAY OF WORKING, PART OF ITS BUSINESS CONCEPT.

Involve individuals and groups into discussions before making important decisions. This does not necessarily mean that everyone is involved and takes the decision, but that the relevant people can present opinions to help shape the decision before it is made.

On important topics it is useful that several people comment before the boss takes the decision. I am not suggesting you have voting, as in an association, or try to reach consensus.

The idea is to have a group of relevant people help the manager make a better decision. This is extremely useful as they can offer different viewpoints, different approaches, and they feel involved in the company.

An English expression explains it.

"The group is *making* the decision, but the boss is *taking* the decision."

The opportunity to influence important decisions regarding their work is extremely important for many people. To be constantly told what to do can work at first, but rarely holds up in the long run.

Many managers feel that they involve their employees in their decisions. Unfortunately, employees often see it as a technique in which the manager

40

is trying to make employees feel involved when, in fact, the decision has already been made.

How, then, should you go about involving people in a decision? Involve relevant employees in decisions that are complex and would benefit from more than one point of view. The result will be both better decisions but above all, decisions that get implemented.

Dr. Ichak Adizes[1] for more than 40 years has developed and practiced a common-sense management philosophy that seeks to address effective decision-making and good implementation. His process is designed to achieve good decisions while also building mutual trust and respect in the group, making this is a very strong methodology.

To use this approach, the first step to solving a complex problem, is to gather those who can *influence* the quality of implementation, have *relevant knowledge* about the problem and - of course - the person who has the *formal right to take the decision.* The group will together explore the problem and propose a solution. The decision-maker then takes the decision - and is responsible for the implementation. This significantly improves chances of implementation since the key people affected by the decision have been included in the decision and had the chance to influence it.

Now what happens if the manager who has the authority to take the decision does not agree that the decision reached by the group is the best for the company?

First, this happens very rarely. The manager was involved in the full discussions during the decision-making process. Most managers realize the importance of having key people in the decision-making and that this is worth a lot in implementation. By the end of the decision-making process, differences in perceptions about how to implement have been addressed in the give and take discussion, and people key to implementation commit to moving forward. But should this happen, it is the manager's right as he or she is accountabe for the results, not others in the group.

---

1.   See for example, Adizes, I. K. (2016). *Mastering Change - Introduction to Organizational Therapy.* Adizes Institute Publications: https://store.adizes.com

## HOW ABOUT EFFECTIVENESS?

The manager who makes his or her decisions alone, while others who will implement think the decision is wrong, soon realizes these decisions are ineffective. This individual approach to problem-solving is a major source of "resistance to change."

I am sure you have heard countless examples of managers making and enacting decisions on their own who have limited success with implementation. Numerous management teams have testified this to me over the years.

*Making decisions is a children's game, but getting them done and implemented is closer to an art.*

As an added benefit to this participative decision-making, we can also get motivated employees with increased trust and respect among each other. This builds a strong team, even if it takes a little longer in the actual decision-making. Still another benefit is implementation from committed people who made the decision will happen faster.

Use of such a *management approach* can have a dramatic effect on both companies and employees and helps to end the never-ending focus on financial compensation for employees.

An employee's ability to influence the task and the company increases motivation, well-being, and commitment.

# 6. FINANCIAL REWARDS

Now we get to the third type of rewards, which are the financial incentives. This final step in creating a reward system is the one where too many managers start. By doing so, they usually make their incentive systems more expensive than they need to be. And often they don´t really motivate the employee.

Some examples of financial incentives include:

- A CEO receives an extra million dollars because the company has reached a certain profit level
- A Marketing Manager receives an extra two months' salary for opening a new market in Eastern Europe
- A product manager gets an offer of options in the company for opening a new production line in one of the factories

If there is a logical connection between a performed action, the company objectives, and the size of the reward, this works relatively well.

Of course, there is always the risk that other employees' frustrations grow as they wonder, why not me? This is especially true if they played a role in reaching the results being rewarded.

This is difficult to guard against, but one important tool is transparency. People should know a specific person has the opportunity and that there is a clear link between the company's goals and the achievements and results that the individual or group is tasked with.

Financial rewards can vary considerably, both for the scope of expected work and the size of the reward. The most common reward is simply money - a payout when, for example, the year is over and you can see the result.

To help build transparency and trust in a financial reward system it is imperative to have everything clarified in advance. A simple but important example is whether the payment includes any social or income taxes.

Shares or options can be distributed if the company achieves certain goals. The shares can then be sold after a certain specified time so that payment in cash need not be so large at first.

One prerequisite sometimes used is that the managers also buy shares. For each purchased share, an agreed number of shares may also accrue to that person. The number of shares accrued can depend on whether the company has achieved certain targets or goals, for example:

The return on capital employed or how well the company has performed in relation to competing competitors, etc.

The manager can then sell the shares on the market, or he might be bound to keep these shares for a certain period.

## 6.1 WHEN WILL THE REWARD BE PAID?

Should the reward be paid out at year end? Or as soon as the result is known?

Once a year is the usual time for paying the reward. Be aware that the more often you pay the reward, the sooner employees learn how to manipulate the system. A common example of manipulating the system is to postpone sales into a next period if a salesperson has already reached quota for the current period.

On the other hand, shorter reward periods can increase satisfaction because of the higher frequency of payments.

## 6.2 FINANCIAL REWARDS/BONUSES

As discussed previously, the corporate world uses rewards as recognition for good performance. Rewards are given in the form of money or praise including greater responsibility, a promotion, or some other intrinsic reward.

Beyond just recognition, though, the reward is also intended to increase the individual's motivation.

The greater motivation is expected to increase performance and loyalty to the company or some other desirable behavior. Key to effectiveness of rewards is job content. When a person's work is laborious and monotonous, praise usually gives little internal motivation, so the individual asks for more money.

You might argue that it is more logical to ask for a more interesting task than to ask for more money. After all, do you want to continuously work in a boring task even if you are paid more? A person probably asks for money because it easier than trying to redefine her job into something more interesting. After all, the person is doing what she was hired to do, and job design was never intended to be one of her responsibilities.

If a worker's internal motivation is small or does not even exist, then you will have to pay more compensation. If, on the other hand, the intrinsic reward is high (when the work is interesting and offers development opportunities) the need for financial compensation is less and often *significantly less.*

If the work is not interesting and does not offer challenge and opportunity, people only do what they think is possible, that is, ask for more financial compensation. And to make things worse, people will do as little work as possible or only what is required to complete their task. Even when they receive extra compensation, it likely will not be perceived so much as a reward but only what they should have gotten in the first place for the boring work.

*The conclusion is: people who like what they do, will do it even when they get paid less. People with boring work will ask for more money to compensate for what they perceive is missing in the job.*

## 6.3 CONSTRUCTION OF A BONUS SYSTEM

Before building a good reward system we need to understand the needs the system must fulfil.

Start by clarifying what are the important and critical activities in the organization right now? Is it sales? Is it production or maybe finding new people in key positions?

By first identifying the primary driving activities we understand where we should focus a rewards and bonuses system. If your company has identified "Key Performance Indicators" or KPIs these can help. Be warned, though, managers often create KPIs just to have something to measure. They will work well as a basis for rewards only if they have been developed with a focus on truly 'key' activities.

Next, you will need a measuring system in which you can link an individual's or group's performance to their goals or to the important KPIs. You need to decide what type of reward to offer - money or something else that is perceived as valuable.

The reward needs to be interesting enough for the individuals involved to focus their efforts. The reward also needs to be linked to the interests of the company.

Here are some other important questions which should drive the construction of a reward system:

- Should the reward include only certain individuals and if so, which ones?
- What level of reward is planned?
- What should be the mix of financial and non-financial reward?
- Should there be a "cap" on the financial reward?
- How and when are the rewards distributed?
- What lifetime will the reward system have - 1 year or until further notice?

Reward systems can easily become a "habit." They are difficult to start but even more difficult to end. So, please, to make your life easier, set a time frame for when the reward system will be re-evaluated.

Reward systems are one of the critical elements in your company you need to get right, and they will grow in complexity as your company grows. In the following chapters we will dive into some of the detail for creating a system.

# 7. DIFFERENT FORMS OF FINANCIAL REWARDS

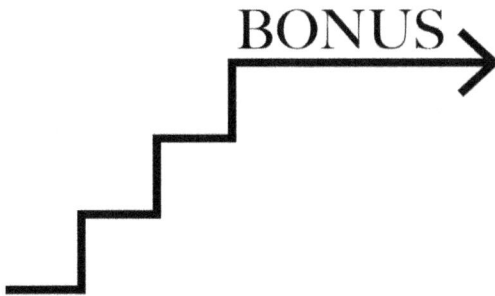

BONUS →

## 7.1 BONUS, PROFIT SHARING, GRATUITY, OR COMMISSION

A **bonus** is compensation agreed on up front and paid to a person or group when a result is achieved.

**Profit sharing** is paid based on both performance of the individual or group and the positive financial results of the company.

A **gratuity** is a reward that is determined after the outcome is known. A gratuity is usually linked to salary and the amount of the gratuity is decided at the end of a defined period.

A **commission** is a variable reward that is considered as a part of the regular salary and paid based on achieving certain results usually linked to sales amounts.

## BONUS

A bonus is a reward that has been decided in advance and awarded to an individual or a group after the achievement of a defined goal.

With this method a person always knows where he or she stands compared to planned outcomes. This may seem like an obvious system, but many employees do not understand what is expected of them or, if they do, they do not have the ability to fully influence the achievement of the goal set for them.

## PROFIT-SHARING

Profit sharing is a type of reward that relies on two levels of achievement – performance of the employee or group and profit of the overall company. Only reaching one of the targets will not trigger the reward. Clarity and transparency are vital in this system. In addition to having clear and specific goals, people need to know the company's profit, what level of profit will trigger the reward and what amount of the profit will be shared with whom.

Explicitly linking profit-sharing to achievement of specific performance goals is important. Otherwise, it is left to the discretion of management if and how the profit is shared. This increases uncertainty among staff, which can lead to frustration and decreasing motivation. Also, with this uncertainty you are slipping into the next type of reward, a gratuity.

## GRATUITY

A gratuity is best known as tipping the server after a nice meal in a restaurant. Corporate rewards can also come in the form of a gratuity. This means the granting or withholding of a gratuity is left solely to a manager's discretion the same as a customer leaving a tip when happy with the received service.

Management will decide if a bonus is given, and which employees or groups will get which amounts. Nothing is decided in advance including on what specific criteria a gratuity is given or in what amounts. The gratuity is certainly received positively when it is handed out. For example, an unexpected Christmas bonus is a form of gratuity. One risk with this type of gratuity is that the link to specific achievements during the year is usually nonexistent.

Another risk is that once a gratuity is awarded it can quickly become an expectation for the next period. The thinking becomes "since we received a bonus last year why shouldn't we get it this year as well. After all, the company is making a profit."

## COMMISSION

While bonuses like profit sharing and gratuities are perceived as an add-on to the salary, the commission is considered more as *part of the salary*. Awarding commissions is most common with sales personnel who can receive fixed salary, plus a commission based on the sales results they achieve. In some cases, the entire salary can be a variable commission, meaning you only make money when you make sales.

In the table below you can see the mix of these different reward and how they are typically applied throughout the organizational hierarchy. Fixed salaries on their own are usually used lower in the hierarchy. Commissions can be used throughout the organization. Bonuses are used higher up where you can affix individual or group responsibility for results. Sharing in the company's profits or a department's contribution to profits is usually used among senior managers.

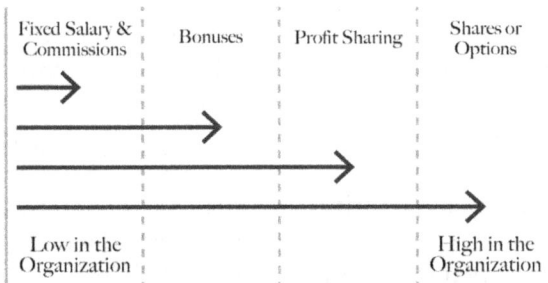

49

Finally, receiving options or shares is usually for a few people in leading positions. Of course, there are exceptions here too.

You can also combine the different forms of rewards. Here again, the higher up in the hierarchy, the greater the chance of opportunities with combinations in all areas from the picture above. A Managing Director may have a fixed salary, a bonus based on certain results, receive a certain portion of the profit, and have shares or options available.

A word of caution here. Young companies should not go into profit-sharing prematurely. As many of you know, young companies are not likely to have much in the way of profits. Early-stage companies should offer more variable pay in the form of bonuses for company development or your own unit's contributions and commissions for sales.

However, in more developed companies, profit sharing is very applicable. If your people are working hard to build your company's success, they should share in that success.

*Make clear which behaviors or results a bonus system should enhance in the organization. Only begin to construct the bonus program after that insight.*

## 7.2 THE "FORM" OF THE REWARD

Fixed salary, commissions, bonuses, a share of the department's contribution, and profit-sharing are all disbursement of money. Options and shares are not directly linked to money but can be exchanged for money, although sometimes with a delay.

There are, of course, variations on the money theme. Deferred option allocations, investments in the company's shares, favorable purchases for the reward money. But these are specialized tools and not widely used.

A good financial compensation system can consist of the following parts:

- Base salary including fringe benefits - we will return to that concept
- Commission – usually as the variable part of a total salary
- Bonus awarded for a completed task or achieving expected results

- A share of the unit's contribution over a specified level
- Profit sharing on the results of the whole company
- Options or share allocations

For each level to work, these aspects also need to be considered:

Is it possible to measure the result?

Is the reward for a group or an individual?

Can you estimate the level of bonuses?

Will the payout period be annual or something else?

Once you have answered these questions you will be ready to construct your reward system.

## MEASURABILITY

For your reward system to be considered fair, it should be based on various measurable results. This can, though, be carried to the extreme. If you focus solely on objectively measurable results, the ability to reward certain activities and behaviors is limited. For example, if it is vital to develop and conduct a sales training to increase sales, it is difficult to measure the impact of the training on sales and the quality of the training is quite subjective. You can, however, simply verify whether the training took place and quite often verification is the best you can do.

*Objectively measurable results* are of course a simple thing to use. You can measure sales in euros, costs in different areas, inventory turnover, personnel turnover, profits, equity, borrowings, etc. for all eternity.

The advantage with objective measures is the ease to determine a quantifiable result. Too often, though, this happens without there being any discussion about the measurement's relevance to important activities.

Using measurable results, we need to decide in advance the specific targets, the amount of reward, and how it is distributed.

## AN EXAMPLE:

We have budgeted for a profit of €1.2 million over the next period and we reach €1.4 million. The target was exceeded by €200,000.

Perhaps we decided ahead of time that 10 percent of any amount over the budget of €1.2 million will be given as a bonus to the group with a maximum of €100,000.

Therefore, the bonus will be €20 000 to be split by the group.

Sometimes management decides that the variable bonus kicks into effect at, say, 90 percent of the budgeted amount. In this case, then, the bonus is triggered at €1.08 million and the amount eligible is €320,000. Now the 10 percent bonus to be split is €32 000. This scenario most often occurs when the fixed salary is set lower than the market average with the assumption that the variable pay will fill the gap.

This latter example, however, contradicts one of my basic tenets. A budgeted amount is a goal, and the fixed salary should be compensation for reaching that goal. Any variable pay is added on to the fixed salary when the actual result exceeds the budget. As well, any variable add on that will be awarded for exceeding results must be defined before the period starts to avoid conflicts.

But there are no rules without exception. A goal might be set that is lower than the budgeted amount for some legitimate reason. An example could be that the fixed salary was set at a lower level compared to the competitors, so you decided a bonus starts at 90 percent of the budget.

## BINARY RESULTS

Often situations arise in which results are not objectively measurable and we need to reward them.

Examples can include:

- Opening a new market where the objective was simply to enter the market
- Building and launching a new website
- Introducing a new IT system that works
- Successfully negotiating a merger with another company

- Hiring a key person to fill a long empty position

In each of these cases, we need to link a reward, such as a bonus, simply to the completion of the action. But we cannot yet know how the action will positively impact the company. All we can do is to verify the action was completed. This is a binary action as it has either been implemented or not. *A binary result can easily be as important to verify as an objectively measurable result is to track and may need to be rewarded when completed.*

## AN EXAMPLE:

For a long time, management has been saying a sales training is needed for our 12 salespeople. We finally set a goal that for next autumn two, 2-day training sessions must be completed. The person assigned as responsible is the sales and marketing manager.

A bonus is set with the understanding that if the training takes place and the sales budget is met then €3,000 will go to the sales and marketing manager.

The training has been completed and the sales budget is met. Thus, a bonus of €3,000 goes to this manager.

## ANOTHER EXAMPLE:

A senior manager in a company had agreed that a bonus of three-monthly salaries would be awarded when a new performance evaluation process was launched and the unit reached its budget. Both criteria must be met.

Both of the above are examples of binary situations: either the task was met or not. Nothing is said about percentages above budget or some other measurement – just yes it was done or no it was not.

## SUBJECTIVE RESULTS

*Subjective results* complicate things even more. Examples of subjective results would be we want to "improve confidence and trust" in the company; or we need to "improve the relationship with a key supplier during the next six months"

However important these tasks are, they are not easy to measure. Should we remove these from our bonus system?

I do not think so.

These can be key areas for improvement. The best we can do is an approximate assessment of how things have changed, perhaps by asking the opinions from a couple of employees. This approach is better than to not consider it at all for a bonus.

However, you need to be aware that the more you rely on subjective assessments, the greater the demands placed on trust and respect in the company. If the trust and respect among people is low, then subjective assessments are not going to be viewed as reliable. When thinking about subjective assessments you can follow the adage, *"it is better to be approximately right than to be precisely wrong."*

## AN EXAMPLE:

A weak relationship between the sales and warehouse departments has long troubled the company. Customers facing delays with deliveries and shortages in inventory have led to tensions between the two departments. Both units blame each other, and it is important to resolve the problems and work together to do the best for the customer.

A plan is drawn up in which the warehouse manager and sales manager are given the responsibility to improve the relationship between the departments.

To measure progress, everyone agrees that after the autumn period, a survey will take place with at least half of the employees in each department and several customers.

If the management team, based on the questionnaires, sees that improvement has taken place, a bonus of up to €4,000 will be distributed between the two managers or based on their recommendations, to others who contributed to the improvement.

This bonus is based on both objective measurable results and subjective recommendations. Subjective recommendations may be based on a binary result, which means a task or program was either completed or not.

## 7.3 INDIVIDUAL OR GROUP

A bonus system can be based on

- An individual's performance
- A group and their results
- The results of the entire company
- Combinations of the above

Managers tend to feel that a bonus should be individual. An individual delivers good results and should be rewarded accordingly. This may be appropriate and could provide strong motivation, but it is not always possible to attribute performance improvement to an individual.

A group effort may lie behind good results even if only a single person was responsible. This can apply to sales efforts, the introduction of new IT processes, training of different staff groups, a move to new premises and many other examples. In cases like these in which groups are involved, rewarding the responsible individual is common and often perceived as unfair. At these times you should consider how to reward the group.

Rewarding group performance can be both positive and the right thing to do. Strengthening team collaboration is a strong motivator and reduces the risk that an individual bonus creates discord, jealousy, and poor cooperation.

Opening new markets, launching training initiatives, designing and implementing marketing projects are all examples of efforts by groups to achieve positive change. They should be rewarded as a group.

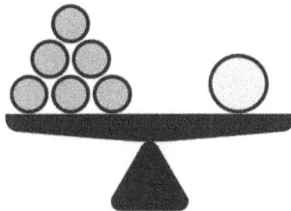

Reward a group or an individual?

### *Reward a group or an individual?*

Large companies often use some form of profit sharing to reward all staff in the company. Usually, different reward amounts are set and distributed for different positions and often without clarity on how the amounts were set. Using this approach also makes it difficult to link the bonus to achievement of specific goals.

As with individual rewards, group rewards should be set ahead of the performance period and linked with specific results and targets.

# 8. REWARD LEVELS

Determining the level or size of the bonus can create long discussions and sometimes a lot of irritation. If we set a relatively low base salary compared to competitors, it is easier to have a more generous performance-based bonus resulting in higher overall compensation. Managers will like this approach, yet many employees feel insecure with the lower base salary.

Too overcome the resistance, management may keep the bonus open-ended, meaning the reward can grow to unlimited amounts. Many managers who initially felt confident in their predictions leaving bonuses uncapped, later found they had to pay large amounts as situations change. Financial headlines are rife with stories of vast amounts of bonuses paid to CEOs, elite financiers, and others. Stories of companies doling out millions of euros in rewards appear regularly in the news and spread negative and greedy images of companies, individuals, and bonus-systems.

To avoid these situations and escape paying excessive bonuses, you should consider setting a maximum amount, so a bonus has a cap. A bonus cap can be constructed in several ways. You might set a maximum amount in euros or perhaps a set number of monthly salaries as the bonus; an example could be two monthly salaries rewarded annually.

Another possibility is to cap the bonus at a certain percentage of profits or sales.

## CONSIDER THIS EXAMPLE.

The management group in a listed company had a bonus based partly on company profits (25 percent) and partly on sales development in a new market, Brazil (75 percent). The bonus was planned to be about €5,000 to each of the seven in the management team. However, to be safe a maximum amount of three months' salary was stated. The average salary was about €8,000 per month.

Sales in Brazil turned out to be a huge and unexpected success driving the bonus per management team member to €50,000 each. The cap, though, kept the bonus at three monthly salaries or about €24,000. A bonus on profits was not even considered as the cap had already been reached by the bonus on sales development. By capping the rewards, the company avoided an exorbitant sum of reward while still giving the management a sizable bonus.

A word of warning. When considering bonus systems such as these a wise approach is to consider linking the reward to profit rather than sales growth. Most managers know that growing sales and flat or declining profits is not uncommon. Giving a bonus for growing sales while profits are not growing can be dangerous.

## BASE SALARY

To have greater flexibility in bonus discussions, the ideal would be that the fixed part of the salary is set about 20 percent below the market level. Of course, this is not always possible. But getting close to this gives you room to negotiate a good bonus plan. The final agreed plan then can look something like base salary at 80 percent of market level with base plus bonuses reaching 120 percent of market level. A model such as this, when agreed to by the employee, provides good incentive for improved results.

When starting discussions on bonuses, you will most likely already have a system of wages in place close to, or even above, market levels. You may find it is not possible to just drop to a base salary 20 percent below the market level. In this case, you must work with what you have and start slowly. In this scenario, the bonus amounts will be lower to begin with.

When designing the variable salary, you may also include some important fringe benefits.

## FRINGE BENEFITS

Another part of rewards can be fringe benefits. These are valued benefits that are given rather than cash, e.g., training, travel, or health insurance. While cash payments can be tax-liable, fringe benefits often reduce the tax burden for the employee.

Sometimes the company gives out trips - perhaps in the form of next year's annual conference at a nice holiday resort. Of course, any tax agency rules must be followed – for example, a certain number of hours per day must be spent in the conference - but the opportunity is still attractive.

More examples of fringe benefits can include travel to fairs, foreign customers, regional training; tickets for events; a paid membership at a health club; or a company car.

A key to having an effective fringe benefit program is that the reward should link to an employee's interests. The problem here is we rarely know what feels interesting, encouraging, and important for each employee. Then, how do we design personalized benefits if we have hundreds of employees.

One way that companies get around this, is to offer a catalogue of benefits from which an employee chooses what he or she likes. Then based on performance the employee can earn credits or points towards earning that reward. A word of warning here is that you need to check your local tax laws as in some countries giving gifts in this way can be considered tax evasion.

Of course, fringe benefits also cost the company money. But when used effectively they can also give employees rewards that are often as valued as simply receiving more money.

## BASE SALARY AND COMMISSION

Commissions are usually linked directly to sales made. For each product sold or for every specified amount of money earned, the employee gets a certain percentage of the sale. This means salary and commission have been negotiated as a combination in the normal salary. Both sides understand that a certain commission is part of achieving the right salary level. Thus, the commission does not add to the salary for well-executed performance but is included in the normal pay package. In these cases, there is rarely any cap or restrictions on earnings potential for the salesperson. The commission also is almost always an *individual commission.*

Quite often, the total salary is based on a relatively large commission so the person can obtain an acceptable salary level. In example 1 below, the commission and base salary are about the same and represent an acceptable salary amount.

In Example 2, the individual's sales are significantly smaller, the commission consequently less. The total remuneration, if it continues at this level of salary plus commission, will likely not be enough and unsatisfactory for the individual.

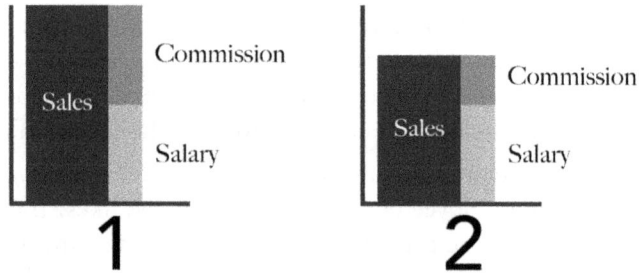

*The payout schedule* in this example is usually that the commission is paid at the same time as the base salary, thus monthly. It is possibly with a one-month lag for the commission, so sales amounts can be collected before paying the commission.

## SALARY AND BONUS

As has been written above, the most common form of variable pay comes as an addition to the base salary as a bonus. The bonus *adds extra to the base salary*, where the salary itself is considered full compensation for the work done.

The bonus should then be an extra boost to get something extra for an achievement beyond what is expected. By only achieving set goals employees should not get the extra compensation. An additional result should be required.

Then the question becomes what is the "additional result"? Next we will map out some ideas in this area.

# 9. BUDGET AS A STARTING POINT

As a manager, you start a period by creating a budget. You will create projections to achieve a certain sales result or maintain a certain cost level for a specified period, for example, over the next month, season, or year. This budget becomes the basis for discussions on bonuses. Should your employee exceed the sales budget or finish below the budgeted cost level then this is a good starting point for a bonus.

## 9.1 BONUS LEVEL – WHEN SHOULD A BONUS BE AWARDED?

Achieving budgeted results should not be enough for bonus payments. That achievement should be accommodated in the base salary! Bonuses should be based on *improvements*, not just for achieving set budgets and their goals.

In example 1 in the next page, the individual has achieved budgeted sales and accordingly receives his based salary.

In example 2, the individual achieves higher sales than budgeted and, in this case gets a bonus in addition to the salary for the amount above the budget.

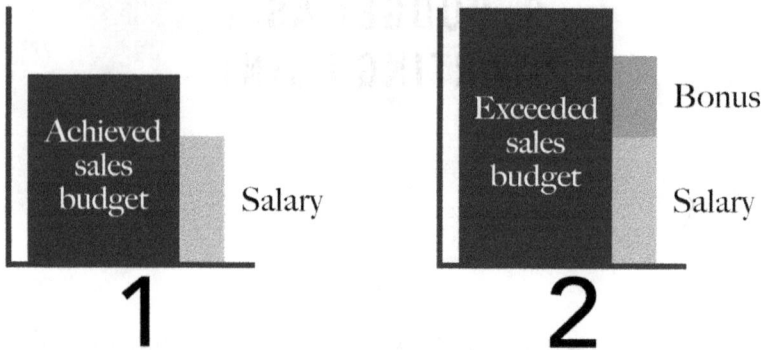

For this example to work, we need a measurement method. With sales, it is easy to measure how much the individual exceeded the budget. If we are working to save costs, measurement is also straightforward.

If, we look instead at carrying out an activity - conducting a large market survey, a training activity, or reducing inventory - there may be other things to be measured.

Sometimes it is just counting the number of items in inventory, or it could be a binary measurement, which means yes or no that the task was completed.

When tracking goals, it is possible the goal will change over time and become lower than in the original budget. Market changes may have occurred during the year and the goals needed to be updated. In this case, the budget remains the same and the changed goal can become the starting point for the bonus.

## 9.2 SIZE OF THE BONUS

When a person produces such results that a bonus becomes relevant - how much should the individual be able to earn? You can "scale" the result so the more achieved the higher the bonus or make it binary, i.e., you get €1,000 or you get nothing.

In a binary system, even as sales or cost savings increase, the same fixed bonus is paid out. End of discussion.

## AN EXAMPLE OF A BINARY SYSTEM:

Again, looking into a sales department and comparing budgeted results with actual results we can see how this works.

Example 1 below shows the amount of budgeted sales. Example 2 shows that the budget was exceeded and an agreed upon bonus was paid. In example 3, an even greater result was achieved. In the binary system, though, only a fixed bonus is available and remains the same despite achieving a better result!

You can also scale the bonus based on the result. As an example, if the budgeted result was agreed at €1,500, the bonus can start at say, €1700. When the outcome is between €1,700 and €2,000, 10 percent of the extra result (€300) is received as a bonus; so, €30 if €2000 is reached.

If the results are even better, you can scale the bonus, so the salesperson receives 15 percent of everything above €2,000. Thus, at a result of €2,400 the final bonus would be €30 for the amount up to €2,000 plus €60 for the additional €400. In total, a €90 bonus.

## 9.3 DISTRIBUTION OF THE BONUS

When we move to group bonuses, we need to decide how to split the reward. Should everyone in the group have the same amount? Or should the amount of reward differ for each person based on some criterion? Regardless of the split agreed upon, the plan needs to be discussed in advance of the work being done.

Here are several ways to split a group bonus:

- Equal distribution to everyone.
- Distribution in relation to each person's salary.
- Distribution according to task, e.g., a visiting salesperson might get twice as much as the shop salesperson.
- Distribution depending on contribution to the result.
- Distribution depending on the group's opinion who contributed what.
- Distribution based on the manager's opinion who contributed what.
- Any other predefined distribution.
- A combination of the above.

You can see this topic will likely require many discussions and is a potential source of strong disagreement. This will be especially complicated if you have not discussed and agreed on the system in advance of carrying out tasks and distributing bonuses.

In the example below, six people have been given the opportunity to share an end of year bonus for their team over-achieving results. When the time comes, the manager receives an allocation of 40 percent of the result. One key employee gets 20 percent of the bonus, the other four employees get 10 percent each while the manager gets 40 percent.

Fair? That is another discussion. But hopefully this split of the bonus has been discussed and agreed on in advance.

Here is another example of a reward amount for distribution in a small company, a department, or among a team.

The amount of bonus to be awarded based on results and shared by the unit's members is €18 000.

- The manager receives €7 200 (40%)

- A key person receives €3 600 (20%)
- 4 employees each receive €1,800 (10% each, 40% total)
- Total amount reward €18,000

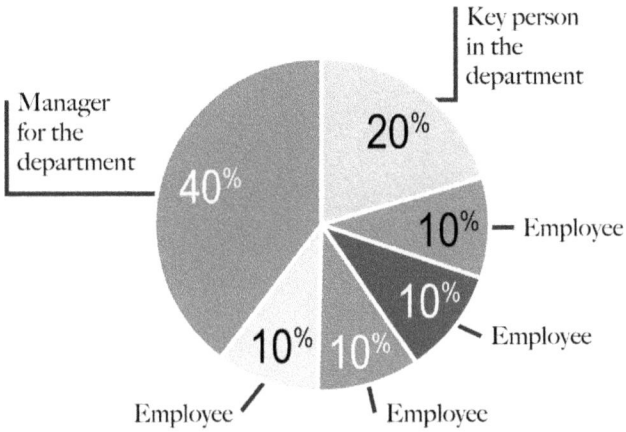

*Example of a Group Bonus distribution*

# 10. WHAT SHOULD
# BE REWARDED?

The chapter title might also have been formulated: On what results should we build our reward system?

There are, of course, many areas to choose from when selecting a suitable base for your reward system. Companies in different stages of development have different priorities and need to invest their time and resources in appropriate areas.

In his book *Managing Corporate Life Cycles*[2], Dr. Ichak Adizes defines ten different stages of company development – each stage has different characteristics and different priorities to deal with if they are to move forward in a constructive way.

We will go through two of the different stages, covering the young fast growth company and the aging inflexible company, to see how their differences affect reward systems.

## 10.1 OBJECTIVES IN THE GO-GO
## STAGE OF AN ORGANIZATION

During the early growth period in a company's development, the *Go-Go* stage, Dr. Adizes describes how the company, brimming with confidence from its new-found success, often enters diverse business areas having very little to do with the core business. An example is a manufacturer and retailer of

---

2.   Adizes, I. K. (2004). *Managing Corporate Life Cycles*. Adizes Institute Publications: https://store.adizes.com

body care products which had quickly reached global success. The founders, brimming with over-confidence decided they could also handle the hotel business and the gourmet chocolates business.

Quickly establishing operations in these two industries, they nearly lost the company. Employees complained that the company direction was unclear, they did not know who is responsible for what and virtually everything from the three companies had to circulate around and through the founders.

Often this divergence gets the company into trouble. Because of the youth of the company, the routines, systems, and administrative procedures are all underdeveloped. The *Go-Go* company simply does not have the infrastructure and managerial capacity to deal with the increased complexity.

In this stage of growth, the company should concentrate and focus its efforts on customers, products, and product development. Initial investments should aim at building market share, opening new markets, and steadily improving operations through optimized administrative systems, reduced inventories, streamlined functions, and many other internal development issues. Any company needs to master its current business, both facing the market and in internal operations, before jumping into another business. The adage 'do not bite off more than you can chew' aptly applies here.

To encourage efforts in mastering the core business, key people must have goals aligned with the right initiatives. From these goals are derived key performance indicators or KPIs and then rewards are paid for achievement of the KPIs and goals.

Examples of KPIs for such a *Go-Go* company might include:

- Reduce the total number of customers by 200 to maintain focus on the regional market
- Reduce the number of products by 20 percent
- Introduce a new reporting system to determine the profitability of each product line

With the help of these goals and KPIs, you will begin to build discipline and efficiency in the *Go-Go* company. Management will determine which products are the most profitable and which are losing money. As well, with the implementation of standard operating procedures, the professionalization of the company begins. The successful results of a company being run with systems, processes, policies and on-going problem solving, rather than the whim of the founders is the development of a management team that can manage the company supported by the founders.

Once *Go-Go* companies have the management 'infrastructure' in place, a reward system can be designed to reinforce achievement of the set goals and KPIs.

Another stage of the company's lifecycle Dr. Adizes calls *Aristocracy*. Having reached its peak of success, a company falls into aristocracy because it has begun relying too heavily on its past achievements. Management has strong administrative systems in place and the company is likely showing good profits, but the generation of new ideas and new products has declined sharply. The entrepreneurial spirit has waned. The mentality of the company has changed from playing to win to playing not to lose.

## 10.2 OBJECTIVES WITHIN ARISTOCRACY

At this stage, it becomes vital to rekindle innovation and entrepreneurship. Some important objectives will be to find new markets, innovate new products, and pursue new business ideas. Goals should circulate around what is missing by encouraging new initiatives, new ideas, decentralizing, and building new subsidiaries.

Some real examples can include:

- Establish a company in Denmark with twenty new Danish customers next year.
- Introduce two new products next year
- Start a new subsidiary in e-sales next year

71

## HOW TO SUPPORT INITIATIVES WITH BONUSES

The aristocratic company must develop new strategic and tactical goals around innovation and change. How can bonuses strengthen and clarify these goals?

If we look at the company's strategic goals - perhaps for a three-year period – the aristocratic company will need such goals as:

- Sales should grow by 70 percent during the period.
- Do not drop below a margin of 7 percent.
- An internet sales unit for company products should be launched and account for at least 20 percent of the company's turnover by the end of the period.
- Lean certification of at least 40 percent of the company's production department employees must have been completed before the end of the period.
- A new geographic market will be opened in Norway, which will account for at least 10 percent of the company's turnover at the end of the period.

The goals above are simple to formulate and should be supported with measurable sub-goals. Goals in units sold, financial margin, and internet sales are usually measured as a number or euros or a percentage of improvement.

Certification is a typical area that becomes a binary measurement: either the certification is completed or not.

Opening a new market in Norway can be interpreted in two ways – first, that you simply start sales in Norway and, second, that a certain percent of sales is reached.

## 10.3 BONUS WITH THE HELP OF KPIS (KEY PERFORMANCE INDICATORS)

Key performance indicators are the benchmark measurement for areas that are currently of great importance to the company. As we pointed out before, KPIs can vary greatly and, unfortunately, are not always visible in a budget. As well, KPIs have become something of a catchphrase for measuring everything the company is doing. The important idea is you measure only activities that are key to the company's success. For example:

- Sales of a key product that is currently of great importance to the company
- Investments in a key market where the number of customers or sales is of great importance
- Cost reduction in an area that may be in crisis right now
- Training in an important new technology or to gain critical knowledge
- Comparing number of hours charged in relation to available hours
- Sickness absence compared to previous period.
- Reducing certain stocked products
- Introducing a new data solution in the company

A virtually endless number of variants and possibilities can measure performance. You must choose carefully to monitor those items that are vital to the company's performance and development at this time. That means KPIs will change as priorities change. A single budget will not capture each of the areas above. Therefore, the risk is that we will not pay enough attention to these areas. Raising them in the relevant bonus discussions can remedy that shortcoming.

## EXAMPLES OF BONUSES ASSOCIATED WITH KPIS

Let us look at a few examples.

For a regional company, gaining momentum in the northern Sweden market is key to this year's success. Positive progress in this objective is defined as sales of more than €1.2 million for the next year.

A concluded agreement is that the unit responsible will receive a 5 percent bonus, €60,000 to share when reaching the target. This measurement is binary; either the team reaches the target or not. By the end of period, sales were at €1.45 million. The team reached the target and the €60,000 was paid. The agreement had capped the bonus so nothing extra was rewarded for surpassing the goal.

## ANOTHER EXAMPLE:

A computer company's equipment leasing service had stalled at 50 to 55 percent usage of leasing time available.

To increase the usage, the company set a KPI to reach 70 percent usage and billing. The agreement was that once this target was reached a bonus would be paid and the responsible unit with eight consultants would share about €12 000 - 8 percent of the excess revenue on the charge to the customer.

The reward system also had a scaled bonus that made available more than €12,000. The group of eight succeeded to reach a 72 percent usage rate, which resulted in €177,500 additional revenue for the company and a bonus of €14,200 for the eight data consultants to share.

## ANOTHER EXAMPLE:

A small company with about 300 employees created a bonus system in which everyone would be able to participate. The bonus was divided into two parts with one part based on the company's results and the other on each department's results.

For the company results, management set a scaled bonus based on EBITDA - earnings before interest, tax, depreciation, and amortization. The company would pay bonuses when EBITDA reached €2 million above the budget with a cap set at €4 million above budgeted EBITDA.

When reaching €2 million above budgeted EBITDA, €1,000 would go to each employee with a rising scale up to a maximum of €2,000 when the company reaches €4 million above budgeted EBITDA.

The department bonuses would only be paid if the company reached its budgeted EBITDA. Each department bonus was based on its budgeted earnings and on fulfilling 4 out of 5 Key Performance Indicators unique to each department.

If the department budgeted level is reached and 4 of 5 KPIs achieved, then each employee also would be paid an additional €2,000 bonus. Smaller bonuses were also available should a department partially fulfill its KPIs. Thus, a total of €4,000 is available to each employee.

To repeat, though, *no* bonuses would be paid if the company did not reach its budgeted EBITDA. As well, the additional department bonuses would not be paid if the department did not reach its budgeted earnings level.

# 11. WHAT SHOULD WE NOT REWARD?

This question may not always come across the bonus designer's table. But it should.

Bonus discussions are often run by habit. This means that there are often constructions around turnover and profit. While these are necessary considerations, with a little more thought it is possible to determine what is of particular importance to the company at this moment.

For instance, a newly started company, as we pointed out earlier, should be focused on sales, market share and growth of its current business model. As well, it needs to begin to build systems, processes, and routines aimed at keeping costs down while building consistency and quality.

But as the growing company becomes successful and is recognized in the market through media coverage, awards, more business, etc. the excitement and energy grow within the company. A result of this enthusiasm is greater confidence and the temptation to grow in directions beyond the current business model because the company leadership sees opportunity for development wherever they look.

While extension of the business model, even diversification into other industries might seem attractive, the company does not possess the management maturity needed to handle the added complexity. This means at this stage of development reward systems should avoid rewarding branching off into new lines of business. Penetrating new markets and developing new products and services in which the company currently has strong capabilities should be encouraged. But avoid the adventures of moving into uncharted waters.

To build management maturity, the company needs to systemize their operations, improve management information systems, and expand participation in decision-making while streamlining the decision-making process.

In short, the company must transition from entrepreneurial management to professional management.

In some cases, this can mean the best course of action is to reduce the company's income by, for example, identifying and eliminating unprofitable customers, products, and services.

*More is not always better!*

At some point management needs to become better at what it is doing. This means investing in internal development becomes more important than only selling more.

In contrast, larger and more mature companies often have lost much of their capability to innovate. These companies need to expand beyond what they are currently doing, explore alternative business models, and generate new and varied income streams. This means they should not reward only maintaining the status quo. But most look for more things to do and develop ways to reward proactive, entrepreneurial behavior.

# 12. WHO WILL BE
# REWARDED WITH WHAT?

We have discussed in general *what* should and what should not be the basis for rewards. Here is a short overview of rewards by position.

- Management and "top managers" should be more focused on medium to long-term, strategic goals of the organization
- At the middle management level, the focus should be on either the profitability or the quality of support and efficiency of their units
- Supervisors should focus on efficiency and narrower, more specific areas of responsibility
- Specialists should focus their efforts on certain production, processes, or products.
- Other employees are rewarded based on the areas they can influence and be responsible for

Different parts and levels of an organization have different responsibilities and the rewards system should reflect that. This highlights my stand *against the idea that one solution can suit everyone!*

# 13. BONUS DISTRIBUTION

When creating the reward scheme, you also need to define the distribution of bonuses among employees.

I have mentioned previously some methods by which distribution can happen. To recap you can split rewards to be:

- Equal for everyone
- Divided in relation to the salary of each employee or
- According to some established principle. For example, by company unit such as warehouse, sales, administration, etc.).

You can also distribute rewards according to how much an individual contributed to the result. An example would be a computer consultant who billed 200 hours gets twice as much bonus as one who billed 100 hours.

But again, it is important that all of this is defined and agreed upon in advance! The level of reward and the reasoning behind it should not come as a surprise.

## 13.1 PART OF THE UNIT'S CONTRIBUTION

Each unit or department that produces revenues should have its results regularly calculated. The calculation should be revenues minus expenses but may also include a portion of costs for services shared with other revenue producing units. An example would be to split the costs of the human resources department and accounting. Then you can look at the results for a revenue producing unit as two possible levels of contribution.

*Contribution 1* refers to a unit's results without including the share of costs for shared services.

*Contribution 2* refers to a unit's results and considers the split of shared costs.

The value of calculating the two types of contribution is that you can measure how well the department is doing on its own through contribution 1 and then measure the efficiency of your support services, human resources, accounting, marketing, etc. through contribution 2.

The two types of contribution also allow you to set certain goals. For example, the person in charge of a revenue producing unit can have a financial goal linked to contribution 2, which includes shared costs.

A bonus can then be linked to the extent that the unit exceeds the planned result of Contribution 2 in the unit. Of course, it is also possible to reward either the unit head or the entire unit based on the improvement in Contribution 2.

If a unit or department is in an early stage of development, it may be better to base the bonus on Contribution 1 in which just the department's own income and costs are calculated without the extra burden of the shared costs.

Later in the department's development, it may be appropriate to switch to the Contribution 2 level as a basis for comparison. When the shared costs are split and charged to each revenue producing unit, a useful pressure arises on administrative units to bring down their costs as those costs will affect bonus levels for other units in the company.

By connecting the bonus to the contribution 2 level you can also have the administrative units take part in the bonus for the revenue producing units. This will serve to increase their motivation to lower costs.

Next, we will look at profit sharing and then return to a discussion on bonuses for groups, individuals, and on distribution of the bonuses.

## 13.2 PART OF THE COMPANY'S PROFIT

The higher you move into an organization's structure, the stronger becomes the case for profit sharing for individuals or groups.

For a CEO, profit sharing is a normal occurrence. Not so normal is for salespeople or other lower-level personnel to share in profits. However, it is not unheard of that profit sharing is extended to an entire workforce, even with several thousand people.

But it is not very common.

As with previous bonuses, profit sharing should only kick in if the company exceeds its planned goal. Often a planned goal is the same as the budgeted result. But sometimes goals for bonuses are created apart from the budget. It can be higher or lower than budget. It may even be that that the company must reach a pre-defined profit level before profit sharing comes into the picture.

Again, there should not be a bonus if the company shows a loss! Bonuses should be paid for performance beyond what is expected!

# 14. CONDITIONS FOR PROFIT SHARING

You should only think about profit sharing when your company has reached a higher level of maturity. In young companies the focus is still on learning the business. Management needs to make sure sales, production, logistics and other areas associated with creating and delivering value are functional. Profit comes later. First you learn how to run your business model and then you begin to optimize it.

When goals are set that will affect bonus discussions and the company is in an early stage of development, the goals should focus on growth of the share of the existing market, introducing related products and service for more market penetration, taking proven products and services into new markets, and gradually improving internal administration and structure.

As the company grows into later stages of development, goals can more aggressively be set to optimize operations and generate profits.

## 14.1 REWARD METHODS BASED ON COMPANY PROFITS OR DEPARTMENT CONTRIBUTIONS

Variable remuneration is not only used to promote short-term results. Yearly results should also be linked to variable remuneration and while connecting it to sales is vital, we need to also consider the connection to profit.

Connecting the profit result to an individual is not always a straightforward exercise - even if the individual is the CEO in the company. But this does not prevent senior executives in organizations from often taking a generous share of the company's profits. They hopefully have contributed largely to the result but in my experience, it is far from always the case.

The profit result, though, can also be linked to a group – e.g. a management team, a business unit, or some other larger group within the company. Of course, the size of the group that can share a piece of the profit can be as large as you like. However, a principle should be that individuals in the group have some influence over the profit level.

As mentioned previously, sometimes profits are shared with all employees throughout the company, even with several thousand employees. The basic idea here is that all employees are important to achieving the result. Still, the size of each person's share of the reward must somehow be tied to his or her relative impact on the final profit.

How to fairly distribute the bonus connected with profit sharing needs to be decided at the beginning of the period to be measured. Usually, a simple approach is taken. For example, a percentage of the profit goes to the CEO and a smaller percentage of the profits to others in the management team.

The risk with such a simple model is that the profit can vary upwards and downwards from year to year, sometimes with quite large variations. The management team can be so focused on building profit in a single year, that they cut costs to the point it becomes difficult to grow the company. In addition, if more people are to be part of the profit sharing, the discussions can fall into fractions of a percent. With a large workforce this can quickly become unmanageable, and it often makes more sense to announce a fixed amount of money for each person's reward.

# 15. PROFIT SHARING
# - A SUGGESTION

Profit sharing works on the premise that a percentage of a company's profit is made available for sharing with employees. This works well when the company has relatively stable profits over time. For companies with fluctuating and hard to predict profits, the challenge becomes how to adapt to changes in profits and the resulting changes in bonuses.

The difficulty with variations year to year is that people who work hard tend to get frustrated because they can never be sure if their hard work will be rewarded.

One way out of this dilemma is to construct a three-year average of the profit and use this to determine the current year's bonus pool. In practice, this means you compare your current year's profit with the previous three-year average. By taking the difference between this year's profits and the last 3 year's average – let us call this difference Delta from the Greek word for difference - we get an amount to use as the basis for profit-sharing.

**An example:**

| Profit year 1 | Profit year 2 | Profit year 3 | Profit year 4 |
|---------------|---------------|---------------|---------------|
| 100 | 150 | 120 | 195 |

The average profit for years 1 to 3 = 123. As the profit for year 4 (current year) is 195 the Delta is calculated as 195-123 = 72.

The 123 is retained in the company and the Delta 72 becomes the amount for profit sharing which can be split into three parts:

- Two-thirds (48) is retained in the company
- One-third (24) goes to the profit-sharing bonus pool

The top two-thirds remains in the company. The other third goes to the profit-sharing bonus pool. This will be distributed to the group that was decided ahead of time would be sharing in profits.

You might distribute only two-thirds of this bonus pool when bonuses are given. The remaining third will be distributed together with the following year's bonus.

Using this model, you achieve a leveling of profits and, consequently, a leveling of the bonus pool across years. You will also limit the incentive for managers to artificially create a single year of higher profits to try and reap short-term gains.

As well, this model provides motivation to stay in the company. Employees who leave will miss out on the retained part of the pool when it is paid out the following year. This can also help to guard against a year where there is no profit to share as they will still get the remainder of the previous year's bonus.

$$\text{DELTA} = f\left( \begin{array}{c} \text{This year's profit} - \\ \text{3-year average profit} \end{array} \right)$$

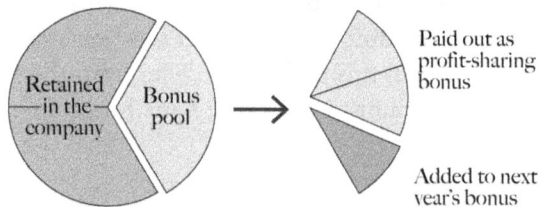

Retained in the company / Bonus pool → Paid out as profit-sharing bonus / Added to next year's bonus

You can, of course, make it even more advantageous to stay in the company by allowing larger amounts of profit sharing to remain for years to come. You can also give out part of that retained bonus in the coming year to employees in relation to their time in the company. Those who leave during the year will lose their share of that bonus. Part-time employees who stay can also receive part of the bonus in relation to their working hours.

By using this type of profit-sharing model, you can see that the company needs three years of profit before even considering profit-sharing. This is good in that it keeps people focused on generating profits for multiple years rather than just the current year.

I will illustrate this with a simple example.

A small company with 100 employees has 65 in production, 15 in sales and 10 in administration. Of the total employees, 10 are in leading management positions.

The first few years of the company's existence they spent finding and securing their place in the market. They developed their understanding of customers and their needs, how to better manufacture products and develop complementary products, how to handle cash shortages, and made and hopefully learned from many mistakes.

After a few years, the company performance has stabilized, and people are optimistic and energized. Profit has been reasonable in the past year and the future looks good. The management decides to test a bonus system.

A simple first year trial of 10 percent of the profits in a pool split evenly among the 10 corporate staff members works well.

Still, as the company has continued to develop and profits are growing, management decides to revise the 10 percent model and they choose to implement the Delta methodology while expanding the bonus to cover all 100 employees. They use the previous three years profits to calculate Delta and apply that against the current year's profit.

Thus, the three previous annual profits in thousands of euros were:

3400

3750

4550

The 3-year average is €3,900,000. The current year's profit is €5,100,000.

Thus, from this year's profits they subtract the 3-year average and get €1,200,000. This equals Delta. This means we have a profit-sharing bonus pool of €1,200,000 and €3,900,000 is retained in the company.

This delta is then split into 3 groups of €400,000 each:

- €400,000 to the profit-sharing pool
- €400,000 to the owners
- €400,000 will be retained in an investment fund in the company

The €400,000 for the profit-sharing pool is what will be distributed to the company's staff. If the company's management so decides, they can also take the next step. They can choose to hand out just two-thirds of the profit-sharing pool this year, while the last third accrues to next year's bonus pool for those who stay in the company. This means that about €270,000 would be available for distribution in the current year and about €130,000 will be distributed with the next year's bonuses.

How the €270,000 will be distributed among the employees is a task that should have been clarified at the beginning of the year. In previous chapters, I presented several possibilities for the distribution from equal to everyone to a breakdown by salary level, by position, or by level of contribution, and so on.

For this example, the company decided on an equal share for each of the 100 employees, which means everyone received a €2700 bonus. The retained €130,000 will be distributed with next year's bonus pool, which will be calculated using the same delta equation as above. Again, before distribution 1/3 of the bonus pool is retained for the following year. The remaining 2/3 plus the retained €130,000 is distributed to the employees.

In this scheme, the management also needs to clarify up front whether the company or the employees will be responsible for paying any applicable taxes.

# 16. PROFIT SHARING - A MIX

We often assume when designing rewards that there is a single best solution for an individual or group. Yet, with some thought we can find ample options to put together combinations of ideas for building innovative reward systems.

A middle manager in a sales department has previously received a bonus based on the results of his department; that is, a percentage of the contribution that the department provides to the company.

This manager is then promoted to the management team. During a transition period, he will continue to work with his sales department while also assuming joint responsibility for the entire company together with the others on the management team.

In this situation, he may still receive a bonus based on the contribution from the sales department and an additional bonus based on the performance of the entire company.

During the first half of the year, 75 percent of his bonus could be based on of the bonus scheme from his sales department role and 25 percent from the performance of the overall company. Within one year, he should have relinquished his sales department role and his entire bonus should be based on company performance.

A company's management can have its bonus built around several temporary parameters other than merely profit. Bonuses can be based on different KPIs regarding staff turnover, customer satisfaction index, liquidity, growth, new market entry, etc.

# 17. AWARD OPTIONS OR ALLOCATE SHARES

You can also make use of the allocation of company shares or the awarding of share options as part of your bonus package. The difference between share allocation and share options is that a person immediately becomes a shareholder in the company when allocated shares. On the other hand, a person awarded options has the right to buy shares at some point in the future at a pre-agreed price and only when exercising that option becomes a shareholder.

Usually, it is only a small part of a company's senior employees who have the chance to be awarded with company ownership. A very few companies, though, have been known to make company ownership available to all their employees.

The compensation mix for top management might include a salary with fringe benefits, a bonus for achieving certain yearly results, a share of the company profit, and the opportunity to receive shares or options.

Often, shares or options are negotiated when hiring a key person, such as a CEO. Of course, this does not prevent opportunities for shares and options being made available to others in the company.

The allocation of shares is a straightforward awarding of a small percentage of company ownership. The price of those shares can then go up or down, resulting in either a win or a loss for the employee. The employee also now has an interest in the future health of the company.

The awarding of options, on the other hand, requires an employee to invest her own money and involves her taking more risk. That investment can be financially rewarding as the person who exercised her option to buy shares can sell later for a higher price. However, the risk is that a person invested his own money which was later lost because the company stock performed badly.

Stock and option deals are not always safe. Sometimes employees lose money. However, keep in mind that when an employee has his or her own money invested in the company, you often get more commitment and greater efforts at improving the fortunes of the company.

# 18. BONUS PROBLEMS?

Any bonus system should be a positive, motivational tool, but it will always come with some challenges. One common challenge is that in times of good company performance, regular bonuses can become expected, even relied upon by the employees.

People get used to receiving a certain level of bonus every period and they eventually take it for granted that the bonus will always be there. Then, when the company experiences a few lean periods and there is no bonus they get disappointed and frustrated.

To help deal with this, a bonus program should change over time. Strategies change, goals and objectives change, and reward systems should also change. By building flexibility into your bonus program, people become used to the idea that the same bonus is not always available.

Another reason to change rewards is that after a while people learn how to manipulate the system, not matter how robust you make it. If the system does not change every year, then at a maximum you need to update it every three years. You will adjust what is measured and how rewards are allocated and distributed.

# 19. BONUS CAPS

Sometimes I hear managers trying to rationalize lowering salaries when results drop. The argument is that if we reward people with more money when things go well, then maybe we should reduce salaries when company results drop. Of course, this will not go over well with employees, and it probably should not be done.

On the other hand, if the company is providing employees a guaranteed minimum salary, it could make sense that employees also get a maximum bonus. Capping a bonus can be done in any number of ways. For example, you might agree on a general rule that no more than two monthly salaries will be awarded. Of course, you could also set a specific maximum amount in Euros, but that becomes more complicated as you will have to calculate the amount per position.

Maybe capping rewards seems like an unnecessary precaution, but too many times predictions are upended. For example, a merger between companies drives sales levels unexpectedly upwards, or a competitor disappears from the market, and you reap the benefits of picking up their customers. Many events can unexpectedly affect short-term sales and earnings results, and sometimes quite significantly. A cap, however, will only take affect with unexpected and significant improvements so when a maximum limit is reached the bonus increase is stopped.

On the other hand, if business performance is bad for some reason, what to do? There should be at least a minimum guaranteed salary. This is especially true if you are placing a cap and limiting how much a manager can earn. Then you should also be ready to limit how little a manager can earn.

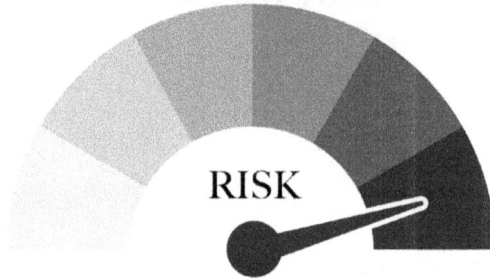

*The lack of a bonus cap will increase a company's risk exposure*

However, when times are so bad that the company's existence is threatened, it may be necessary and prudent to even lower the minimum salary level. If this is done, it must appear as equal and fair. The worst thing you can do is to have salary cuts appear arbitrary or, even worse, favoring some people over others.

# 20. BONUS PAYMENTS

The general principle is that a bonus payment should be made as soon as possible after the defined operating period ends. The period is often one year but could also be monthly or quarterly. You need to keep in mind that the more often you pay bonuses the sooner people learn how to manipulate the system.

Much of the motivation people experience occurs when the bonus payment is close to the posting of results. Another aspect of bonuses is the applicable taxes. Employees will be unhappy if the requirement for them to pay taxes from their bonus comes as a surprise. You must agree upfront how any applicable taxes and other payroll costs are handled. One common approach is that income taxes come out of the employee's bonus amount and social taxes are paid by the company.

# 21. WHY INCENTIVES FAIL?
## LIMITATIONS, GUIDELINES, AND THOUGHTS

The following is a list of eleven points to be aware of that can negatively impact any reward system you create.

1. Under some circumstances a few employees will perceive a reward as offensive. Why would they think that? Because they are already motivated by the job itself, consider themselves doing a good job, and see the reward as a sort rebuke that they need to be performing better. To avoid this type of reaction, discuss up front the reason for bonuses with employees.

However, maybe the employee's performance does need to be improved. An alternative to launching a reward system is to discuss with the employee the results. You should structure the conversation in such a way that you are providing the employee support and development to aid in their growth. Often, the employee does not have the necessary skills or resources to produce better results. Even worse, it may not be clear the results expected from the employee. In these cases, an additional reward is not needed and is unlikely to impact performance.

2. Researchers have known for many years that money is not a good long-term motivator. What motivation money may provide is very short-lived. However, we still expend enormous energy in efforts to use money to motivate.

Mangers probably rely on money to motivate because they know that too little money demotivates. The thinking then, is that more money will motivate people. In fact, all more money does is take way the existing demotivation from being underpaid. While this is important it is not the same as motivation.

Once a fair salary is in place managers also need to know how to construct internal/intrinsic motivators and how to measure their efficacy. Without this knowledge, the only tool left for a manager is money which, as we now know, is very limited as a motivator.

3. As mentioned above, sometimes a financial reward is perceived as too small to be interesting and demotivates people. Management constructed and used a system, but it was designed in such a way that the bonus ends up being tiny as it is split so many ways.

This may be insulting as people feel it would have been better to receive nothing than such an embarrassingly small amount. In this case, maybe it is better to reward fewer people, so others have a reason for working to improve their performance. If this is discussed upfront, it should not pose problems.

4. Confusion and disappointment are virtually guaranteed if you do not agree upfront on the bonus system. You must also agree when no bonus is paid. Any arrangement should clarify that no company bonus is paid unless the company shows a profit. This rule can be a source of consternation. But it needs to apply across the company, even to those units which may have done a good job, while the rest in the company have not lived up to their part. We grow together and we struggle together.

If the company posts a loss, then any profit-making department is obviously disappointed at not receiving a bonus; still the principle should be followed. Of course, exceptions can be made. But it needs to be agreed ahead of time that a specific unit will receive a bonus for reaching its performance targets, even should the company post a loss. An example might be a food production company that is launching a new restaurant concept. If the restaurant is operating under the same company, you might want its management to be rewarded as they are in a startup phase. Whatever the reason, it must be discussed upfront and accepted as legitimate by others in the company.

5. When initially establishing the bonus system you should not combine an employee development discussion with the bonus discussion. The bonus discussion linked to performance should not be a negotiation that includes how to develop individual skills. I prefer to keep the two

separate, because individual growth and skills development should be a regular part of the job and not something a person needs to have an extra reward for.

Growth and skills development of employees must take place on a regular basis. Because of ongoing changes and development in technology and knowledge, if our employees do not grow and develop, our company will fall behind the competition. Therefore, growth and development need to be a part of the culture and not something that is rewarded with bonuses.

6. Do not fall into the trap of thinking that one bonus scheme can fit all employee positions. This is rarely possible. You need to find the right system of reinforcement for different positions as they fill different roles and have different responsibilities.

The lack of bonus differentiation becomes apparent with group or team bonuses. Although, we often should reward a team, realize that the danger is that the high performers can feel slighted if they get the same reward as others on the team.

7. If people are not rewarded for their impact on results, they will grow frustrated. When designing rewards, you need to consider the element of time. The greater the impact a group or an individual has on long-term results, the greater the reason to include profit sharing, share allocations, or options in the bonus system.

The greater the impact an individual or group has on short-term results, the greater the reason for designing variable remuneration including both fixed salary and bonuses based on sales, departmental earnings, or some other measure of performance.

8. A tendency to be aware of is that we become so fixated on establishing short to medium term goals that we lose sight of the long-term strategic goals. Someone must keep those in sight even if they are difficult to measure and track. This is usually the responsibility of the CEO and board.

9. You can have bonuses linked to subjective goals, such as better communication between departments. However, you should have a

few individuals without an interest in the bonus to help evaluate how well the goal has been achieved.

10. No punishment should be applied if bonus levels are not reached!

11. Rewards and bonuses should be as individualized as possible.

And remember:

Fixing areas that people are dissatisfied with does not motivate those people; they will only be less dissatisfied. For example, fixing the heating in a cold office, limiting the amount of continuous understaffing, or correcting workflow problems with a new process will not get people excited to work harder. They will simply stop being frustrated and unhappy. Still, it is important to deal with these dissatisfiers, or they will negatively impact your rewards system.

# 22. WHAT TO CONSIDER WHEN USING FINANCIAL BONUSES?

These are necessary elements of an effective bonus systems

- Bonuses must be aligned with the company's objectives.
- A conscious decision needs to be made about capping rewards
- The company must show a profit - otherwise no reward.
- Be patient as sometimes you will have up to 2-3 years of waiting to see results.

## 22.1 COORDINATION WITH COMPANY GOALS

Company management and key employees must have personal and unit goals directly linked to the company's goals. The executives can and should set their own goals, but only those aligned with company goals should be accepted.

When identifying a company's key activities and setting KPI's (Key Performance Indicators), you are identifying what is vital for the company and on what you will set your corporate goals.

## 22.2 CAPPING REWARDS SHOULD BE CONSIDERED

Too often bonuses grow way beyond what was originally intended. Many businesses experience greater success than what was imagined could really happen. In these situations, designers of reward systems who do not take unexpected success into account will end up paying much more than what was expected. (See also chapter 19 on bonus caps)

For this reason, it may be a good idea to set an upper limit on the reward – a cap. The cap will vary by level. An average cap at middle management is 2 monthly salaries and at the CEO level, about 4 monthly salaries.

## 22.3. THE COMPANY SHOULD SHOW A PROFIT – OTHERWISE NO REWARD

The reward should be an opportunity to share in the positive performance of the company. So, getting a reward when the company is losing money should not be a matter open for discussion. On the contrary, paying extra from an underperforming company will only hasten its failure and must be avoided. Avoiding rewards while the company is losing money becomes

106

more important the higher you go in the hierarchy. You must reinforce accountability for performance.

Even if an individual has delivered a training according to plan, or has introduced a new market initiative, or a new quality initiative, there should be a clause that says, in the event of a loss in the company, no bonus is paid.

## 22.4 SOMETIMES UP TO TWO OR THREE YEARS OF OBSERVING RESULTS IS NEEDED

Launching a reward system is a long-term project. Up to two or even three years may be needed to understand if the system is sustainable. During this time, the awarding of bonuses should be contingent on the efficacy of the system.

As an example, what often happens in the finance industry, is that you fail to reach an objective that looked straightforward. An investment in a financial instrument can initially look good, but after a year or so the result shows that it was not good at all. So, getting a bonus prematurely can be very wrong.

Keeping a part of the bonuses retained with the understanding that it will be awarded if results are sustainable can help here.

# 23. WHAT SHOULD NOT BE DONE WITH BONUSES

The following actions should be avoided in your rewards system.

- Giving bonuses when the company has a loss
- Rewarding the management team while terminating others
- Giving bonuses for results when risk for the company is involved

## 23.1 GIVING BONUSES WHEN THE
## COMPANY IS NOT PROFITABLE

We already covered reasons for not giving bonuses when the company has a loss. A key challenge with not giving bonuses is that those lower in hierarchy who have produced good results have a difficult time accepting not getting a bonus, so it needs to be clearly explained in advance and reinforced.

Beyond the company not having the financial means to spend on additional rewards, the practice can also bring negative attention from the outside world. Customers, suppliers, and the media can all draw negative conclusions towards your management practices, damaging trust, if they see you doling out rewards when the company is losing money.

## 23.2 TO REWARD THE MANAGEMENT
## TEAM FOR DISMISSING OTHERS

Achieving financial goals by firing employees may be mathematically justifiable but is not morally or ethically sound. There are certainly times when companies must cut employees to save costs, but this should not be a basis for a bonus. The practice will seriously undermine trust with employees and when the market hears that bonuses are being given for firing people, there is a risk of serious backlash.

## 23.3 TO GIVE A BONUS FOR OUTCOMES
## THAT ARE A RISK FOR THE COMPANY

In financial institutions, it is not uncommon to see significant, even ridiculous bonuses. Criticism of these practices has grown over the years, not least because they encourage young and aggressive finance managers to take large risks to build up their wealth. Quite often these risks give a company far too much exposure.

An employee's excessive behavior largely occurs because he is risking someone else's money while being rewarded through an uncapped bonus system that he has learned to manipulate. The temptation for fast and large wins becomes too great to ignore.

One solution is to cap bonuses, so temptation is reduced. The difficulty with this is that uncapped bonus systems have become normalized in the finance industry and are now just the cost of doing business. Any company that caps its business system will find itself at a disadvantage when looking for good managers.

Another way to deal with this can be to retain part of any bonus, say 50 percent, for one or more years to be distributed, should the results hold up.

# APPENDIX

The following are examples of results and measures that can be used when creating a bonus system.

Some areas to set goals and measure growth and improvement within the company

- Market share
- Profits
- Quality levels
- Service levels
- Unit development goals
- Revenue
- Number of new customers
- Staff turnover
- Market value
- Combinations of the above

Here are some examples of specific results-related goals

- Establish a new market in the UK
- Increase market share by 5 percent
- Increase profits by 15 percent next year
- Increase sales next year by €600,000 within the Alfa product line
- Reduce the number of complaints to below 3 percent
- Reduce lead time to a maximum of 6 days
- Increase the market value of the company's shares to €12
- Increase the company's value on the stock market to €2 billion

Here are some examples of activity-related goals

- Train all sales personnel in the new sales program

- Introduce a new quality program next year
- Reduce the number of products in the product portfolio by 30 percent during the year
- Launch a new website during the year

The following are examples of financial bonus situations.

## Bonus examples for a company with one salesperson selling service contracts.

The salesperson agrees to a fixed salary plus bonuses based on the following conditions:

- Three percent of new contracts - measured by revenues during the first year from new contracted customer
- One percent on renewal of contracts - measured by revenues during the first year from renewed contract customers
- Annual bonus cap of 4-months fixed salary

The lower percentage for renewal of old contracts provides a reason for the salesperson to follow up and renew existing contracts. At the same time, the effort involved in getting a renewal contract is typically less than for securing a new customer.

In this example, I used revenues as a measure without considering profit. This can be risky and should probably be used only in young companies. Eventually, you will want to reward based on profits rather than only revenues. The reason being that reducing prices is an easier way to sell but reduces profits. Rewarding on profits takes away the incentive to use price reductions as a first step to win a sale.

## Bonus examples for a company with multiple salespeople including salary plus commission

Three salespeople work in a services-based company with compensation that will include individual commission plus team commission.

114

Each salesperson has a fixed salary of €2700 per month – this is below the market-average salary and based on the availability of additional earnings every month from commissions earned on sales levels

The commission cap is €4500 per month for each salesperson. This means a salesperson can have a maximum monthly income of €2700 fixed plus a potential €4500 commission for a total of €7200.

The table below gives examples of different earning potentials on commissions during a month based on sales levels with a sliding percentage for individual commissions. Commissions do not start getting paid until the salesperson reaches €50,000 in sales.

| Ind. Sales | % | Ind. Comm. | Team Sales | Team Comm. 1.5% | Individual comm. with 1/3 of team |
|---|---|---|---|---|---|
| 40,000 | 0 | 0 | 100,000 | 1,500 | €500 |
| 50,000 | 5 | 2,500 | 120,000 | 1,800 | 2500+600= €3100 |
| 70,000 | 6 | 4,200 | 150,000 | 2,500 | 4200+750 ≠ €4500 capped amount |

In the table above, if a salesman reaches only €40,000 in revenues, he gets no individual commission but only his part of the team's commission or €500. If he reaches €50,000, he gets 2500 + 600 = €3100.

Finally, when he reaches €70,000, logically he should get 4200 + 750 = €4950. However, he will receive just €4500 as this is the capped amount.

The advantages to this system are that it is relatively easy to understand, and it offers quick feedback on performance.

The disadvantages are that it is somewhat risky to reward revenues over profits; commissions can vary widely as some months go well and result in high commissions, while down months and low commissions can be demotivating.

However, if the company has developed to the point that it has somewhat predictable sales levels, revenues become more predictable and the disadvantages with low sales commissions can probably be minimized.

## EXAMPLE OF A CEO BONUS

The company has shown a loss for the past three years. For the coming year, the Board decides that a new CEO will have available €100,000 as a total possible bonus. How this bonus is achieved is as follows.

- **€40,000** – This is awarded if the company shows profit at year-end. However, payment of the bonus may not push the company into a loss. None of the following available bonuses are is paid if the company is unable to pay this bonus.
- **€30,000** – This is awarded if invoicing to new customers exceeds €2 million, the profit bonus is reached, and it does not push the company into a loss.
- **€20,000** – This is awarded if Region West shows sales of €400,000 or more, the profit bonus is reached, and it does not push the company into a loss.
- **€10,000** – This is awarded if Region East has at least 5 new customers, the profit bonus is reached, and it does not push the company into a loss.

The important thing here should be obvious. The company must show a profit before any bonus is paid and the allocation of a bonus cannot push the company into losses.

The bonus also has a cap. It is not possible to get more than €100,000. It safeguards the board from possible extreme situations. Perhaps a sudden unforeseen rush on sales that has little to with the CEO's efforts would cause the bonus to reach non-defensible levels.

## A SECOND EXAMPLE OF A CEO'S AGREEMENT

The CEO's fixed gross salary is set at €12,000 per month. A bonus package based on profit sharing is agreed to and specifies the following.

The distribution of any CEO bonus only happens after meeting the budgeted profit level of €840,000.

The bonus is capped at 4 monthly salaries, or €48,000, and the company will pay social taxes, while the CEO is responsible for income tax.

116

The profit sharing is agreed as follows:

| Company earnings: | |
|---|---|
| €840 000 - €1 million | 1% of profits |
| > €1 million | 2% of everything above €1 million |

Therefore, if the company reaches €1 million, the CEO's bonus will be €10 000. At a profit of €1.6 million, the 2% bonus is applied to €600,000 and will provide an additional €12,000 for a total of €22,000. At this rate, the CEO reaches the capped bonus of €48,000 when profits get to €2.9 million.

## REWARDS TO CEO IN A PUBLIC COMPANY LISTED ON STOCK EXCHANGE

When stocks and stock options are added to the bonus scheme, CEO bonus amounts can often exceed 100 percent of the fixed salary. This also means CEOs become owners – and sometimes major owners in the companies they lead. Awarding stocks for performance is a relatively straightforward exercise but can be risky for a CEO. Should the stock price drop, the CEO can even lose money.

Awarding stock options means the CEO will take on more risk because when he exercises the options, he must invest his own money in the company to purchase the stocks. Again, should the stock prices go down the CEO can lose money.

Stock and stock option programs are sometimes combined with other bonuses and can involve substantial amounts of money. Reporting in the media concerning the basis for the size of the rewards is often inadequate and can be misinterpreted as being very favorable to the CEO. The stories you do not read about in the media are those in which a CEO loses when stock prices drop.

Shares and options are also used to convince a high potential candidate to join the company and are often just part of an employment contract, not related to any result other than coming to work for the company.

Some other uses for stocks and stock options in bonus systems include:

- Promoting growth in the share price of public companies
- Promoting growth in profit levels
- Improving performance measured against competitors
- Increasing the return on capital employed
- And any number of other measures

## MIDDLE MANAGERS AND INDIVIDUAL BONUSES

For middle managers, bonus caps are typically set to a maximum of 2 monthly salaries and only awarded if the company shows a profit. Here is a possible mix of bonuses based on a cap of 2 monthly salaries that are not connected to profits or revenues.

- 50 percent of two monthly salaries is paid in bonuses if the new business program works and is used by everyone involved.
- 40 percent of two monthly salaries is paid in bonus if the new quality program is introduced before the turn of the year.
- 10 percent of two monthly salaries is paid in bonus if the fixed costs come in at 5 percent below the budgeted costs.

## SHARE-BASED BONUS PROGRAMS

In 2011, a leading Swedish bank launched a share distribution program for their top management team that ended in 2014.

By the finish of the program, the CEO had received €1.6 million from the program. Together, the four in the management team (includes the CEO) received a total of €5.4 million.

At the start of the program, the four senior managers invested in the program by buying shares in the company at nominal value. Thereafter, they could be awarded up to four shares for each share purchased at no charge, depending on the bank's performance on the stock exchange.

Two-thirds of the reward was based on the bank's earnings compared with the 10-year government interest rate and one-third was measured in comparison with the bank's competitors.

118

At the end of the program in 2014 it turned out that the program paid the full awards of four shares for every share purchased. The company's return was 20 percent while for competitors it was 9 percent and the bank's long-term interest rate was 3 percent.

However, not just the management invested in shares and received dividends. About 500 key people invested €11million, which when the program ended was worth €65 million! A nearly five-fold increase in three years.

Some have questioned whether these large amounts paid out as rewards were ethical. However, these people invested their own money and took on a level of risk as the markets could have gone down. They acted on their own initiative and that means the rewards should be acceptable. However, it might have made sense to apply a cap to the program.

## EXAMPLES OF GROUP REWARDS.
## A GROUP OF SALESMEN IN A WHOLESALE COMPANY

Twenty salespeople covered the Stockholm market. Each had his or her own district but to make sales required a lot of team support. Solving problems and "firefighting" required help from whoever was available, and this often was not the salesperson who had made the initial sale. Also, the sales office supported ongoing contacts of clients as well as monitoring of deliveries. Therefore, all agreed they should have available a group bonus.

The starting point for the bonus was the margin on the sale. Margin was calculated as sales minus the cost of the goods sold, not including fixed costs. On the projected annual turnover of approximately €20 million, a margin of 29 percent was calculated.

This resulted in a budgeted margin of about €5.8 million. Once this margin was reached, 5 percent, or €290 000, would be distributed to the sales team. If everything went according to plan, each salesperson would receive a bonus of €14,500. Social taxes and income taxes would be paid by each employee.

Depending on how purchases, sales, returns, deliveries, and other things went a lot of deviations could occur in this budget. Still, the actual result at year-end would be the basis for the bonus dividend.

## A GROUP OF SALESMEN IN A SERVICE COMPANY

For several years, two salesmen had been employed by the company and were paid individual commissions on the sales they made.

A third salesman was recently hired. In discussions, it became clear that competition between the salespeople could impact results. The two experienced sales guys were ready to help the new hire and introduce him to potential prospects. However, it was obvious that this went beyond their responsibilities and would mean they would have to split their commissions with the new person.

They concluded that best would be to drop the individual commission and instead introduce a group bonus. The bonus system they designed was implemented as follows.

For the first year, total commissions would be divided into five parts. The experienced sellers each received two parts, while the new person received one part. After the first year they will reevaluate the situation, and if it makes sense the bonus will be divided equally between all three of them.

## BONUSES TO GROUPS AND THE WHOLE COMPANY

One reason to give a bonus to a group is that achieving a result is based on a team effort. Therefore, it is only logical that the group shares the bonus.

The question becomes should everyone share equally in the reward. Of course, if you share the bonus equally then problems can arise as people question whether everyone really contributed equally to the result. For example, should salesmen working in the field have the same bonus as those working just in the office on less demanding tasks?

Of course, you can also vary rewards based on levels of contribution, but this can be tough to implement. The difficulty arises because the reward is split only after the results are known and I have repeatedly stated that you should agree why and how the bonus is distributed before the period starts. By using levels of contribution as a determinant for level of reward, you run the risk of people being unhappy with the final split.

**As an example:**

A bonus agreement was made that 25 percent of a group's result would return to the group as a bonus to share. The division of the bonus has not been decided ahead of time because you want to split it according to individual contribution levels. You decided that it would be helpful in this situation to have specific performance measurements. But this can be very difficult. Over a long period (for example, one year), people can make many efforts that affect the outcome which were not foreseen and are not measured.

Therefore, the split of the reward almost always becomes a subjective measurement. Probably the most effective way to deal with it, is to have a system in which multiple people are evaluating performance. One common tool for this is 360-degree feedback.

In some listed companies all employees are rewarded with a share of the profits and in others, employees can participate in a share or option program. However, the bonuses are not always directly linked to any individual or group results or performance standards. Simply a collective reward is established based on overall company performance.

In public companies there are disparities in CEO pay between Europe and the United States. A 2018 report by FW Cook[3] found that median base pay for a CEO in the U.S. is nearly 20% below CEO median base pay in Europe and Australia. However, median bonus opportunities in the U.S. are 175% of base pay, while in Europe and Australia median bonus opportunities are 100% of base pay.

3.   Cole, D., By, Cole, D., (2019, October 11). Comparing Compensation Around The Globe. Retrieved from https://boardmember.com/comparing-compensation-around-the-globe/

**Bo Jäghult** graduated from the Stockholm School of Economics and has worked as a management consultant for more than 50 years. His consulting work has included assignments in most of the countries in Europe, North and South America, as well as across Asia. Bonuses and reward issues have consistently been one of the most important management issues in all his assignments. He has also taught for about 10 years in the Adizes Graduate School in California.

**Greg Mathers** has master's degrees in management from the Adizes Graduate School and Riga Technical University. He has owned and operated four of his own businesses and has been a management consultant and an adjunct professor in multiple MBA programs for more than 20 years.

www.ingramcontent.com/pod-product-compliance
Lightning Source LLC
Chambersburg PA
CBHW072201090426
42740CB00012B/2343